A Complete Guide to Hoysaḷa Temples

A Complete Guide to Hoysaḷa Temples

Gerard Foekema

ABHINAV PUBLICATIONS

abhinav publications

First published in India 1996

Publishers

Shakti Malik

Abhinav Publications

E-37, Hauz Khas

New Delhi-110016

ISBN 81-7017-345-0

Phototypeset in Baskerville 12pt by

Tara Chand Sons

Naraina

New Delhi-110028

Printed at

D.K. Fine Art Press Pvt. Ltd.

Ashok Vihar

Delhi

CONTENTS

PREFACE

For me, enjoying Later Cālukya and Hoysaḷa temples is one of the great pleasures of life. I love these temples because their plans are so logical and natural, because their architecture is so ingenious, and because their execution is so rich. After completing a full scale work on the architecture of Hoysaḷa temples in 1993, it is a pleasure to now present a smaller book for the use of tourists.

More than a hundred of Hoysaḷa temples survive today, and I think more than 10 of them to be of interest to the average tourist. The most important message I have to convey is that the large temples in Belūr and Halebīd give a marvellous impression of Hoysaḷa sculpture, but only a poor impression of Hoysaḷa architecture, because they are seriously incomplete. Visiting a few other villages in the neighbourhood of Belūr and Halebīd is very rewarding, because there smaller but complete temples can be found. Several of these small and modest temples perfectly show the logic and beauty of Hoysaḷa architecture, as is among the well-known temples only done by the famous complete temple found in Somanāthapur.

Amsterdam
September 1994

Gerard Foekema

General

1

WHO WERE THE HOYSAḶA?

The Hoysaḷa were a dynasty of Hindu kings, who ruled a medium sized kingdom in Karṇāṭaka, Southern India, during the 12th and 13th centuries. They began their career as chiefs of hill tribes in the mountains of the Western Ghats. These are the mountains that separate the western coastal belt of peninsular India from the central plains called the Deccan plateau. Karṇāṭaka nearly completely consists of these vast plains; the ghats are low here and the coastal belt only narrow.

Often, in human history, less cultured but pugnacious nomadic people establish themselves as rulers over sedentary people, not seldom adopting a lot of the culture of the ruled. Something comparable appears to have happened in Southern Karṇāṭaka when, during the 11th century, the Hoysaḷa formed a small kingdom in the plains to the east of their part of the ghats, in the region around Belūr and Halebīd. During the 12th and 13th centuries their power extended and provided this region with the prosperity necessary for temple-building. Not provided by the Hoysaḷa, of course, was the sophisticated architectural style of the temples. Their architectural style derived completely from the rich tradition that already existed in Southern India, and that continued in its development during Hoysaḷa rule.

This southern tradition of temple-building is called the *Drāviḍa tradition of temple architecture.* It emerged in the 6th and 7th centuries AD, simultaneously in Karṇāṭaka and Tamil Nāḍu, and reached its first mature achievements in Pattadkal (Karṇāṭaka) and Kānchipuram (Tamil Nāḍu). A continuous line of development connects the Drāviḍa temples found in Pattadkal with the temples built during Hoysaḷa rule. After the fall of the Hoysaḷa kingdom there is, however, a discontinuity in the development of temple architecture in Karṇāṭaka. Though largely situated in Karṇāṭaka, the temples built during the Vijayanagara empire are in fact closer to the temples found in Tamil Nāḍu, and do not continue the character of the Hoysaḷa temples.

2

A SHORT HISTORY OF THE HOYSAḶA KINGDOM

Until the arrival of Muslim forces on the Deccan, in 1300 AD, the political history of medieval South India was a continuous struggle between Hindu kingdoms. There were many of them, large and small, the smaller ones often not being completely independent, but accepting the overlordship of a larger one. The large kingdoms generally had their centre in the northern half of present-day Karṇāṭaka and in the northern half of present-day Tamil Nāḍu. The southern half of Karṇāṭaka was a buffer region between the large powers, occupied by small kingdoms of local rulers. Many of the latter existed only for a short time, but notably one of these dynasties of local kings deserves mention here, because of its exceptional long rule and its high cultural level: the Gaṅga of Talakād. Their capital Talakād is located on the Kāveri river close to the famous tourist place of Somanāthapur, 50 km east of Mysore. During the end of their reign the well-known Jaina colossus at Shravan Belgola, 50 km east of Hassan, was erected.

Let us now start our historical survey at a round year number. In 1000 AD there were two large powers in South India, the Cōḷa of Thanjāvūr and the Cālukya of Kalyāṇa. Both were fresh and full of energy. The Cālukya had acquired power only some 25 years before. The Cōḷa ruled already for about 150 years, but had very recently overcome a period of weakness. Both kingdoms were fighting each other but maintained a balance; nearly all smaller kingdoms were annexed or subordinated. The old Gaṅga kingdom mentioned above had been annexed by the Cōḷa. The 11th century became a period of wealth and great achievements for the heartlands of both empires. Thanjāvūr and several neighbouring cities still bear evidence of this today, by showing the largest temples found in India. Of the city of Kalyāṇa, situated in the north of Karṇāṭaka, nothing is left, but a fabulous revival in temple-building during the 11th century in central Karṇāṭaka testifies to the wealth during Kalyāṇa Cālukya rule. In the region around Gadag temples from every century following the start of temple-building in stone can be found, but in the 11th century their number suddenly increased and a new, luxurious building material was introduced: potstone instead of the sandstone that had been used previously. These potstone temples are very fine and rich, and became the immediate forerunners of the Hoysaḷa temples.

In this political situation of two large and vigorous powers, the Hoysaḷa established their small kingdom close to the mountains, on the frontier between the two large empires. Naturally they could not be independent; they emerged as feudatories of the Cālukya and slowly enlarged their territory with Cālukya consent. For about 100 years they remained small. Only at the beginning of the 12th century they did succeed in becoming important by fighting the Cōḷa and, also, their own overlords. This was done by the first great Hoysaḷa king Biṭṭiga, who assumed the name Viṣṇuvardhana ("prosperity of Viṣṇu") because, not uncommon in human history, military expansion went hand in hand with a religious revival, in this instance due to the teachings of the great Vaiṣṇava reformer Rāmānuja. In 1116 AD Viṣṇuvardhana defeated the Cōḷa governor of Talakād, penetrated very deeply in the Cōḷa territory, and annexed Talakād. To celebrate this enormous success the large Vaiṣṇava temple in Belūr was built and consecrated in 1117 AD. Viṣṇuvardhana then turned against the Cālukya, first with success, but after a lot of fighting, finally, he was forced to again recognize their overlordship in 1123 AD. Nevertheless the position of the Hoysaḷa had changed dramatically: they were a feared military force now, and could consider themselves to be the heirs of the Gaṅga of Talakād. In a festive mood a second large temple was built, now a Śaiva one, in Halebīd. And for the whole area around present-day

Hassan and Mysore, traditionally only a buffer area between large powers, a period of importance and prosperity began. It would last for no less than two centuries. Many potstone temples were built and about one hundred of them, large and small, sound or ruined, are left today. Nearly all of them were originally commissioned by rich citizens: officers, governors or merchants. Only a few were commissioned by the Hoysaḷa kings themselves.

Of course the Hoysaḷa tried to extend their kingdom further, and of course they tried to become fully independent. The latter was achieved by the grandson of Viṣṇuvardhana, Ballāḷa II, also called Vīraballāḷa ("the heroic Ballāḷa"). In the course of the 11th century both of the large empires mentioned above weakened considerably. By the end of the century the Cālukya were seriously attacked by their northern subordinates, the Yādava of Devagiri. Vīraballāḷa joined in, defeated the Cālukya king in 1190 AD and so put an end to the Kalyāṇa Cālukya kingdom. After some time most of its territory was seized by the Yādava, but at least the Hoysaḷa saw affirmed now complete independence. Their kingdom reached its zenith around 1200 AD, and the Belūr-Halebīd region became the undisputed centre of a vast territory. Devagiri indeed is far away, as far north as the present-day city of Bombay.

With the other declining power, the Cōḷa, events took a quite different turn. In the beginning of the 13th century they were seriously threatened by their southern neighbours, the Pāṇḍya of Madurai, and consequently asked the Hoysaḷa for help. The fighting against the Pāṇḍya lasted many years, and in the meantime the core of the Cōḷa empire actually was incorporated into the Hoysaḷa kingdom. Thus, around 1250 AD, the latter included a large part of northern Tamil Nāḍu and then reached its largest size, but only for a short period. The Pāṇḍya continued to grow in power and gradually pushed the Hoysaḷa back to, roughly, the present-day borders between Tamil Nāḍu and Karṇāṭaka.

Then, suddenly, in 1296 AD, the period of rivalling Hindu kingdoms in South India was over: sent by the Delhi sultanate, Muslim armies appeared on the Deccan. At first they came for booty only. In 1311 AD they arrived before Halebīd and the last great Hoysaḷa king, Ballāḷa III, chose to pay tribute to them in order to prevent siege and destruction. In 1320 AD the Tughlak sultans came to power in Delhi, and their aim was to bring South India under political control. Within a short time several Hindu kingdoms, among them that of the Yādava, were defeated. Hindu kings were killed and their princes were sent as captives to Delhi. Muhammad Tughlak started to remove his capital from Delhi to Devagiri, changing its name into Daulatabad. Ballāḷa III decided to keep peace with the Tughlaks and accepted their overlordship, and so Hoysaḷa independence found its end, 200 years after its formation. But still, Ballāḷa III remained a powerful king and would later participate in the Hindu uprising against Tughlak power in the South.

This uprising started in 1329 AD and was soon successfully led by two brothers, Harihara and Bukka. Originally, both of these Hindu princes were taken as prisoners to Delhi and converted to Islam; next they were sent back to the South as governors of the Tughlaks, in order to avert the uprising. But they converted again, back to Hinduism. They managed to unite all Hindu forces and in a new spirit they founded, in 1336 AD, the city of Vijayanagar. This place, its impressive ruins still standing today, was strategically situated in central Karṇāṭaka, in between Daulatabad and the southern half of peninsular India. Ballāḷa III died in 1342, whilst fighting a newly established Muslim sultanate at Madurai. Harihara and Bukka did not give his son the opportunity to assume power. For the first time in the history of South India one large Hindu kingdom enclosing all territory of the region was established: the Vijayanagara empire. The new kingdom introduced a new kind of temple architecture, easily recognizable by its compound pillars and waving eaves, the pillars often containing a rearing animal, and by its quite coarse sculptural decoration. As building material, soft potstone was replaced by hard granite, therefore minute carving is not found in Vijayanagara temples.

And so, the Hoysaḷa kingdom came to an end without having been conquered destructively. The lasting fruits of power and prosperity, many fine temples, are still standing and have suffered only from the ravages of time. Thanks to the interest of science and tourism a large number of them are now safe and well kept. Of the glories and pains of two centuries of Hoysaḷa rule, the expressions of glory have survived, and now attract hundreds of pilgrims and tourists every day.

3

THE DEDICATIONS AND NAMES OF THE TEMPLES

The Hindu pantheon is large, but the overwhelming majority of Hindu temples are dedicated to either Śiva or Viṣṇu. Both deities, however, have many different forms and the names of the temples show a bewildering variety. Nevertheless, all over India, nearly all temples can be considered as Śaiva or Vaiṣṇava. "Śaiva" means "dedicated to Śiva" or "related to Śiva", and the expression can refer to a temple, to a ritual and also to a person. In the latter case that person is a follower or a worshipper of Śiva, and he can express his creed and devotion by painting three horizontal bars on his forehead. Similarly, "Vaiṣṇava" means dedicated to, belonging to or related to Viṣṇu. A Vaiṣṇava devotee can paint his forehead with an emblem containing prominent vertical bars, and often it is reduced to three short vertical bars only, thus forming a complement to the three long, horizontal bars that indicate devotion to Śiva.

In the case of Hoysaḷa temples, Śaiva and Vaiṣṇava temples are about equal in number and sometimes they are found side by side. The large temple in Belūr is Vaiṣṇava, the large temple in Halebīd is Śaiva. Between the two groups the following differences can be distinguished.

Śaiva temples invariably contain a liṅga as the object of worship. The liṅga, a stylized erect penis, is the universal symbol for Śiva. The name of a Śaiva temple often ends with the suffix " ēśvara", meaning "Lord of". For instance, a temple with the name Nāgēśvara-temple is Śaiva; one of the many names of Śiva is Nāgēśvara, meaning Lord of nāgas (snakes). Likewise, Śaiva temples can be named after the devotee who commissioned the erection of the temple. In the village of Koravangala, for instance, there is a Śaiva temple built by a man called Būci, and the temple is called Būcēśvara, Lord of Būci. In the same way, the name Hoysaḷēśvara means Lord of the Hoysaḷa. All of these names refer to Śiva.

Vaiṣṇava temples, in contrast to the Śaiva ones, always contain a cult-image of human form, depicting a special form of Viṣṇu. The temple bears the name of that special form, and never a declension of the name of a devotee or founder. The forms of Viṣṇu most commonly found in the dedications of Hoysaḷa temples are Keśava or Cennakeśava ("the beautiful Keśava"), Lakṣmīnarasiṁha and Lakṣmīnārāyaṇa. The prefix "Lakṣmī" indicates that Narasiṁha and Nārāyaṇa (both forms of Viṣṇu) are worshipped together with the consort of Viṣṇu, Lakṣmī, and the cult-images in these temples show Viṣṇu seated with Lakṣmī sitting on his left knee. Keśava and most other forms of Viṣṇu are depicted standing erect and straight.

In this book a total of 20 temples are discussed; 9 of them are dedicated to Śiva, 10 of them dedicated to Viṣṇu, and only one has another dedication (Dodda Gadduvalli). Finally, in this chapter on dedications, Jaina temples should be mentioned. Being non-Hindu these temples are neither Śaiva or Vaiṣṇava, but enshrine a Jina, a naked hero standing in meditation. They are not many in number among Hoysaḷa temples, and none of them is beautiful enough to be included in this book.

4

THE PLAN OF THE TEMPLES

Hoysaḷa temples consist of several parts, but these parts are always connected to each other and form a unity. They are, therefore, the complete opposite of many famous temples in Tamil Nāḍu, which often consist of different parts standing loose from each other. A Hoysaḷa temple is just a single building, often consisting of one cella and one hall only. The cella contains the cult-image and is entered by the priests; the hall is for the devotees to gather, to perform pūjā and to watch while the priest performs pūjā on their behalf. The hall can be of two different kinds: open or closed. In between hall and cella there often is a vestibule. Before the entrances to the hall there frequently is a porch. No further parts are to be found in a Hoysaḷa temple. Consequently, taking into account the two different types of hall, there are only five different temple parts: cella, vestibule, closed hall, open hall and porch. We will now discuss each of them in some detail.

The part of the temple that contains the cella is called *vimāna,* the best English term for it is *shrine.* The vimāna usually bears a tower and is therefore easily recognizable. Its inside forms a strong contrast to its outside: the inside is simply square in plan with plain walls, hence the name cella, the outside is complicated in plan and is profusely decorated. The outside plan is a star, a staggered square or a combination of star and square, and consequently the walls show many projections and recesses. Each projection of the wall has a complete architectural articulation with many decorations. Notably the top of each projection is crowded, and these tops are repeated several times in the tower. Often, a visitor unfamiliar with temple architecture will just notice a rhythmical jungle of decorated projections, recesses, blocks and mouldings. This chaos is only illusory; a strong and logical order is present but difficult to perceive, because the Hoysaḷa architects often intentionally made the vimāna as complicated as possible. Analyzing and explaining that order is beyond the scope of this book and, perhaps, the Hoysaḷa architects did not intend for visitors to understand it; simply attracting attention to the most important part of the temple probably was their aim.

The inside of the vestibule is similar to that of the cella, it is also square and plain, and it is of an equivalent size. Its outside walls are decorated but inconspicuous since they are only a short continuation of the walls of the shrine. It also has a tower, which is a low protrusion of the tower of the shrine, and therefore it is called *śukanāsī* or *nose.* In Hoysaḷa temples the nose is often crowned with the beautiful Hoysaḷa crest, which consists of a royal warrior stabbing a lion.

Like the shrine, the *closed hall* has thick walls and no windows, only entrance openings. Naturally it is larger, and therefore it has four central pillars supporting its roof and dividing it into nine compartments or *bays.* Both inside and outside of a closed hall are square in plan, and in this case not only the outside but also the interior bears decoration. In the inside, it is the four pillars and the nine ceilings that are usually the most beautiful; often the pillars are lathe-turned and often the ceilings are very intricately carved. On the outside its walls are a continuation of the lower part of the shrine, often with a less complicated architectural design but always with the same rich decorations. Never, in a closed hall, there are more then 4 pillars and 9 bays; consequently, a closed hall is always modest in size.

The other kind of hall, the *open hall,* is very different from the previous kind. Its plan is not a square but a staggered square, and here the number of pillars and bays may vary (Figure 1). Often this plan is called "cross in square", but that name is only adequate in case of the smallest form consisting of 13 bays. The peculiar thing about open halls is that they can be larger, even much larger. The walls of an open hall consist of a parapet-wall only; resting on this

Fig. 1

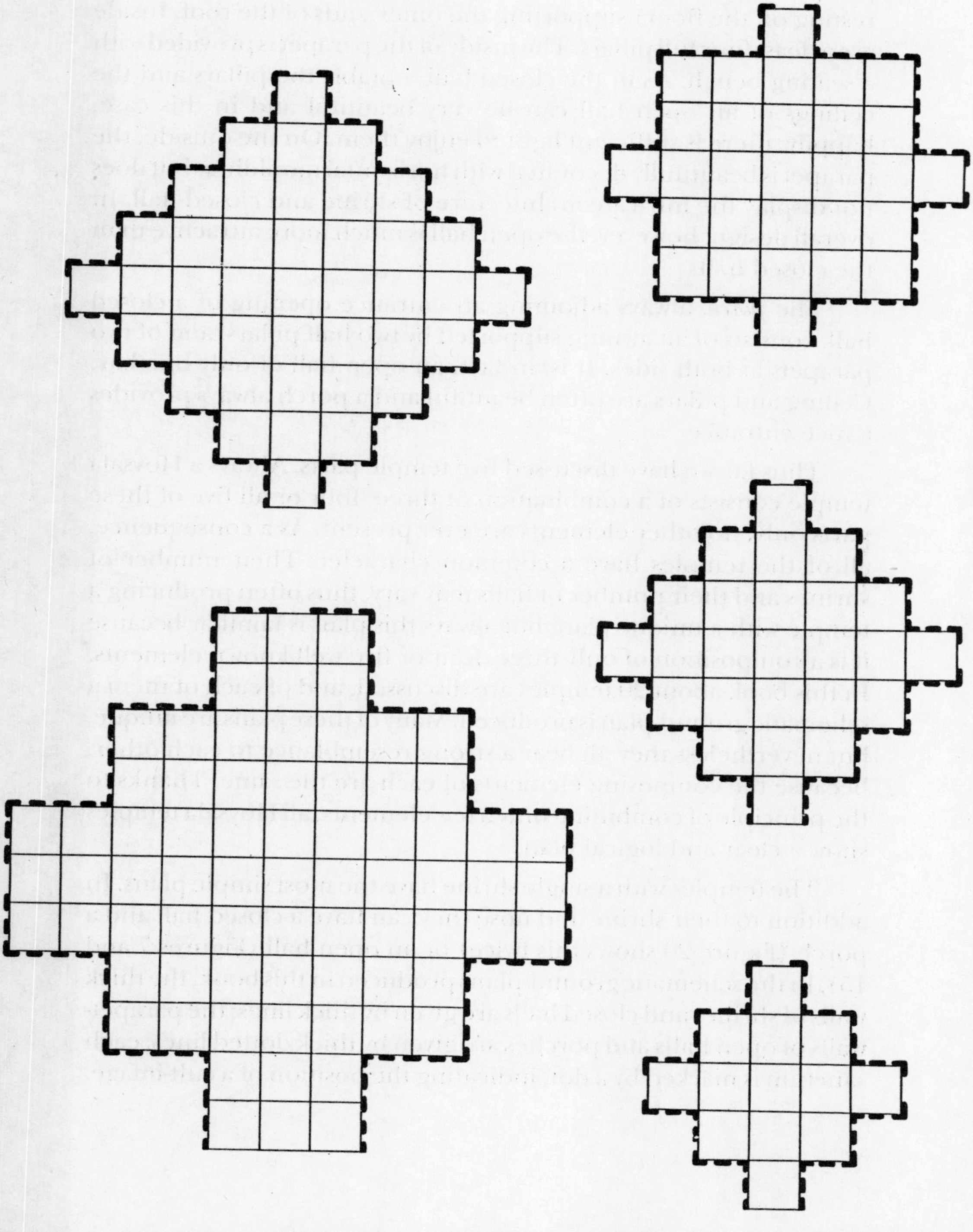

parapet are half pillars (their length is about half of the pillars resting on the floor) supporting the outer ends of the roof. Inside are at least four full pillars. The inside of the parapet is provided with a seating bench. As in the closed hall, notably the pillars and the ceilings of an open hall can be very beautiful and in this case, happily, there is sufficient light to enjoy them. On the outside, the parapet is beautifully decorated with horizontal mouldings but does not display the intricate architecture of shrine and closed hall. In overall design, however, the open hall is much more attractive than the closed hall.

The *porch*, always adjoining an entrance opening of a closed hall, consists of an awning supported by two half pillars, and of two parapets at both sides. It is, in fact, an open hall of only one bay. Ceiling and pillars are often beautiful and a porch always provides a nice entrance.

Thus far we have discussed five temple parts. Always a Hoysaḷa temple consists of a combination of three, four or all five of these parts only, no other elements are ever present. As a consequence, all of the temples have a common character. Their number of shrines and their number of halls may vary, thus often producing a temple with a unique plan, but always this plan is familiar because it is a composition of only three, four or five well-known elements. In this book about 20 temples are discussed, and of each of them a schematic ground-plan is produced. Many of these plans are unique, but nevertheless they all bear a strong resemblance to each other, because the composing elements of each are the same. Thanks to the principle of combining only a few elements, all Hoysaḷa temples show a clear and logical plan.

The temples with a single shrine have the most simple plans. In addition to their shrine and nose they can have a closed hall and a porch (Figure 20 shows this twice) or an open hall (Figures 7 and 15). In the schematic ground-plans produced in this book, the thick walls of shrines and closed halls are given by thick lines; the parapet-walls of open halls and porches are given by thick dotted lines; each sanctum is marked by a dot, indicating the position of a cult-image.

A temple with one shrine has only one tower and is called an *ekakūṭa* (one top). Apart from the types with one hall it can also have two halls, in that case a closed hall is always preceded by an open one (Figure 2 and the upper half of Figure 9).

Temples with two shrines are called *dvikūṭas* (two tops) and show greater variation in their plans. The two shrines can be positioned beside (Figure 11) or opposite each other (Figure 18), and each possibility can use closed halls, open halls, or both. Temples with three shrines, called *trikūṭas* (three tops), show less variation, because the three shrines are nearly always arranged around one single hall (Figures 5, 12, 14, 16, 17, 21 and 22). Often in Hoysaḷa architecture only the central one of the three shrines has a tower, and so the term "trikūṭa" is not always literally true. Temples with four (Figure 10) or five shrines do exist but are rare; they are made up of the same temple parts as the others and, consequently, also show regular ground-plans.

Finally, a chapter on plans should mention the platform of many Hoysaḷa temples. This platform could be considered as temple part number six because, besides underlining the beauty of the temple, it has a religious function: the function of *pradakṣiṇā.* Performing pradakṣiṇā means the circumambulation of a shrine, always in clockwise direction, and is an important form of worship. Architecturally, the platform always forms a perfect unity with the temple, because it carefully follows the outline of all temple parts.

5

SCULPTURE

In Hoysaḷa temples architecture and sculpture go hand in hand, because the architectural design of all temple parts has been achieved mainly through chiselling. Of course the sculptors produced decorations, but they also executed architectural articulation. Since architectural shapes can be both functional and decorative, it is very difficult to separate architectural sculpture from purely decorative sculpture, and we will describe both of them here, starting at the top of the temple and slowly descending to its base.

The highest part of the temple is the tower topping the shrine; on top of this tower there should be a large and beautiful water-pot, called *kalaśa.* Often it has been lost in the course of the centuries and is replaced by a metallic pinnacle; without any exception such a metallic finial is a later addition, originally there always has been a *kalaśa* as shown in Plate 40. On top of the adjoining nose there can be the Hoysaḷa crest, consisting of a royal warrior stabbing a lion. Not all temples have them and, though certainly a number of them have been lost, it seems probable that not every nose was originally provided with one.

Below the kalaśa, the top of the tower of the shrine is formed by a very large domed roof which resembles a helmet. In fact it is not a dome but a solid structure, which consists of large stones sculptured in the domed form. This is the largest sculpture found in the temple, its ground-surface can easily measure 2 by 2 metres. Always it is a marvellous piece of sculpture, beautifully shaped and finely decorated. It is square in plan when the shrine itself is square; if the shrine has the plan of a star, its plan is the same type of star.

Below this giant topping roof, the tower consists of many more domed roofs with square plan, all of them much smaller, and also crowned by kalaśas. They are mixed with other small roofs of different shapes, most of them finely decorated. The top of the wall of a closed hall also shows this kind of decorated miniature roofs, but only one single row of them, and also above the heavy eaves of open halls and porches one row of them can be found. The tower of the shrine mostly consists of three or four of this kind of rows, the top of the nose mostly of two or three of them.

Below the superstructures just described there runs an eaves all around the temple, mostly it is very heavy and projects half a metre or more. Below this eaves two different architectural and decorational schemes can be found. One of them is very close to the temples that were built before Hoysaḷa times and the other one was introduced during Hoysaḷa times, we will thus name them "Old" and "New" here. Common to both schemes is the presence of decorative towers on pilasters and of large images of deities and their attendants. In the *Old kind* of temples, the wall-images are placed below the decorative towers, and below the wall-images the base of the wall consists of a set of 5 different horizontal mouldings, one of them a row of blocks. In the *New kind* of temples there is a second eaves running around the temple, about one metre below the first one; the decorative towers are placed between the two eaves, and the wall-images below the lower one. The base of the wall consists of a set of 6 equal rectangular mouldings, each of them of the same width. This New scheme was originally introduced in the large temple in Halebīd, but only much later did it become a usual way of shaping and decorating temples. Generally speaking it can be said that temples dating from the 12th century are of the Old kind, and temples dating from the 13th century can be of both kinds but, if elaborate, they mostly are of the New kind.

In both kinds of temples the decorative towers, each resting on one or two slender pilasters, can be very different in quality. Sometimes they are beautiful, sometimes they are odd or slovenly. Always beautiful, however, are the large wall-images. Especially in the New kind of temples they often form a continuous row all around the building and can easily number more than a hundred. On the Śaiva temples, all gods of the Hindu pantheon can be found; on the Vaiṣṇava temples, however, forms of Śiva are usually absent. Identifying all the images is very difficult, but a large number of them can easily be recognized; this will be the subject of the next chapter.

Below the row of large images there is the base of the temple. In the Old kind of temples the horizontal mouldings of the base, usually 5 in number, each have a peculiar shape of its own, and mostly they are left without any further decoration. In the New kind of temples the 6 rectangular mouldings of equal width are always sculptured, they therefore are called friezes. From top to bottom they show birds (haṅsas) in the first frieze, *makaras* (aquatic monsters) in the second, epics and other stories in the third, a vegetal scroll in the fourth, horses in the fifth and elephants in the last frieze. In the scroll and between the makaras the face of another monster, called *kīrttimukha,* often appears. The epic frieze is the most exciting, because it shows scenes from Hindu mythology and from the two large Hindu epics, the *Rāmāyaṇa* and the *Mahābhārata.* Visitors should note that the sequence of these scenes is opposite to the one found in modern comic strip books! It runs from right to left, in accordance with the direction of pradakṣiṇā.

In this discussion of decoration we have distinguished two types of temples, the Old kind and the New kind. There is, however, a third kind that seldom occurs, but should here be mentioned briefly. In this third kind of temple, the projections of the walls are not framed by the usual long and slender pilasters, but are instead given the shape of heavy square pillars. In contrast to the other Hoysaḷa temples, architectural shapes derived from architecture in wood are absent. In addition to this, the tower of the shrine, if present, has a completely different character. This third kind is called *Nāgara* because it derives from the temple style of Northern India.

6

RECOGNIZING THE MOST IMPORTANT DEITIES

The most striking sculptural decoration of many Hoysaḷa temples is a horizontal row of wall-images of gods and their attendants. The study of the meaning of depictions is called "iconography". The iconography of Hoysaḷa temples is difficult, but just recognizing a large proportion of the icons is quite easy. With only a little knowledge, easily more than half of the depicted gods and goddesses can be identified. The aim of this chapter is to provide non-Hindu visitors with that knowledge.

Forms of Śiva have four or more hands bearing, among other attributes, a trident and a peculiar kind of small drum. Exactly the same small drums are often sold to tourists; they are shaped like an hour-glass and produce their sound when twisted. If a male icon shows both trident and this kind of drum, it can only be Śiva; if a female icon does, it can only be his female counterpart. Often Śiva is depicted dancing, often slaying a demon, and often enjoying the company of his consort Pārvatī and his bull Nandi. A god depicted naked always is Śiva. Special depictions of Śiva found on Hoysaḷa temples comprise the following: dancing on a demon: Śiva slaying Andhaka; dancing on the head of an elephant and holding its skin up behind his back: Śiva slaying Gajāsura; standing almost naked with his genitals clearly visible, with a spherical hair-do of small curls and wearing sandals with high heels: Śiva as Bhairava.

Forms of Viṣṇu always show a wheel and a conch. If a male icon shows these two attributes it can only be a form of Viṣṇu; if a female icon does, it is his consort Lakṣmī. In all he has four attributes:

wheel, conch, mace and lotus-flower, and often he is depicted standing straight and showing all these attributes clearly. The four attributes can change between his hands and, because the number of different sequences of four elements is 24, this produces 24 slightly different icons; each one has a name of its own. On most Hoysaḷa temples many of these slightly different depictions of Viṣṇu are found, and on some temples all 24 can be seen; the most popular among them is Keśava. Besides these 24 forms, some of the 10 avatāras (descendations) are often depicted; Viṣṇu descended to earth 10 times in order to rescue or to do justice, each time in a special form. Special depictions of Viṣṇu found on Hoysaḷa temples comprise the following: seated on the coils of a snake: Viṣṇu with Ananta; seated with a female on his left thigh: Lakṣmīnārāyaṇa; the same with the head of a lion: Lakṣmīnarasiṅha; seated, with the head of a lion, pulling out the intestines of a demon lying in his lap: Narasiṅha avatāra; with the head of a boar, walking over a demon: Varāha avatāra; with two hands only, playing a flute, lifting a mountain or dancing on the head of a serpent: Kṛṣṇa avatāra, respectively Veṇugopāla, lifting Govardhana or slaying Kāliya. Finally two short stories showing Viṣṇu deserve mention, each consists of two sculptures found beside each other: the right-hand sculpture of the pair showing a king (umbrella) and a small figure, the left-hand sculpture showing Viṣṇu taking a giant step with a stretched leg: Vāmana avatāra; the right-hand sculpture of the pair showing a god riding an elephant (Indra), the left-hand sculpture showing Viṣṇu with Lakṣmī on his thigh and seated on the shoulders of a winged man (Garuḍa): the stealing of the pārijāta-tree.

Besides forms of Śiva and Viṣṇu, many other gods and goddesses can be found, and also a few other figures may receive a full image of their own, notably the winged mount of Viṣṇu, Garuḍa, and one of the heroes of the Mahābhārata, Arjuna, the latter always in the act of shooting the fish. All these images are alternated with attendants, females with two hands holding a fruit and a fly-whisk. Sometimes full sized musicians, mostly with a drum, occupy the place of an attendant. Deities other than forms of Śiva or Viṣṇu found on

Hoysaḷa temples comprise the following: a god with an elephant's head, seated or dancing: Gaṇeśa; a god standing straight with two hands only, holding symmetrically two times a lotus-flower: Sūrya; a god riding an elephant: Indra; a god with four heads and beards (three of them visible): Brahmā ; a goddess with a small bundle of paper, a noose, an elephant-goad and (but not always) a long musical instrument: Sarasvatī.

Finally two icons should be mentioned that show exceptions to the rules mentioned above for Śaiva and Vaiṣṇava icons. A goddess with numerous hands carrying all kinds of attributes, including trident, wheel and conch, killing a buffalo, is Durgā ; in order to slay this special demon, all the gods gave her their weapons. A god standing straight and holding both a trident and a wheel and conch is Harihara, a combination of Śiva and Viṣṇu.

The Temples

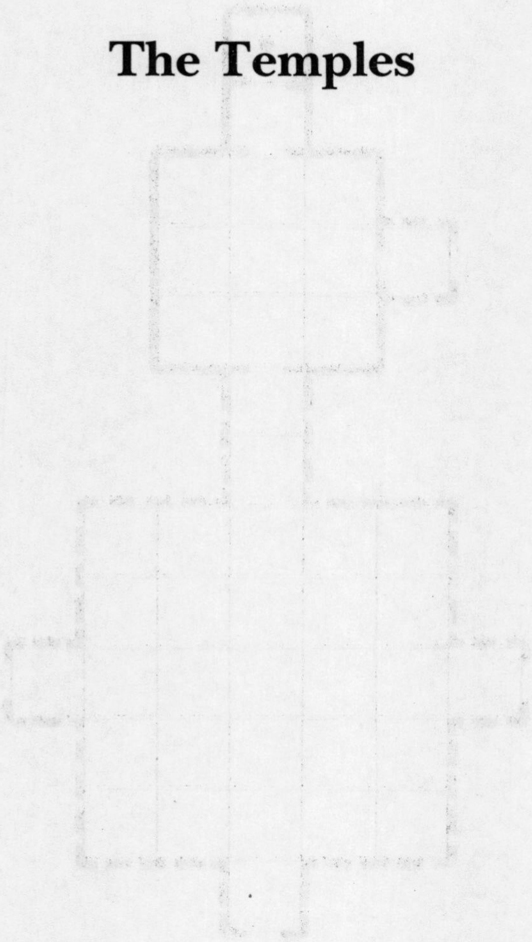

Fig. 2

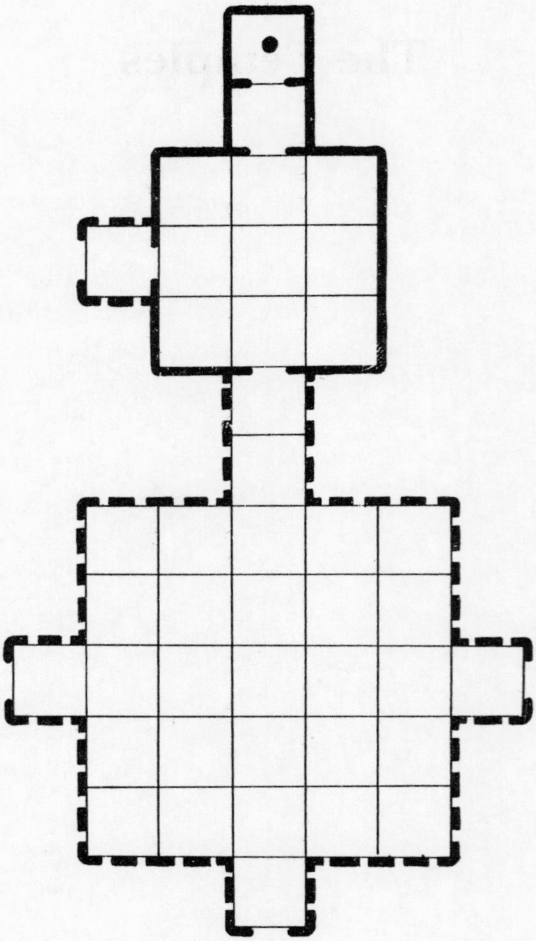

1

AMRITĀPURA

Amritāpura is situated close to Tarikere, about 110 km from Hassan and 35 km from Shimoga. The Amṛtēśvara-temple found here is a first class tourist attraction, because it shows both fine architecture and fine sculpture. All of the temple is beautiful, but it especially is the large open hall that deserves attention. The monument dates from 1196 AD and is well conserved. It is surrounded by an original compound wall and by meadows beautifully maintained by the Archaeological Survey of India. Only the modern props that are needed to support the very heavy eaves mar its view.

The Amṛtēśvara-temple has one shrine and two halls. Next to the shrine and its nose, there is first a closed hall consisting of the common 9 bays, and a porch at its southern side. Then, next to the closed hall, there is an open hall of 29 bays and one additional bay connecting it with the rest of the building. An open hall of this size is a rare marvel, the only comparable one can be found in Belvādi.

The shrine is simple in plan, square with three projections per side. It is complete with its original tower, only the kalaśa on top of the tower is missing. But on top of its nose, the Hoysaḷa crest is present! The decorations of the many miniature roofs of the tower are very fine and well preserved. The walls are decorated with towers on pilasters and vertical scrolls. The base consists of 5 traditional horizontal mouldings. Thus the decorational scheme is of the Old kind, only large wall-images are missing.

The closed hall has the same execution and decoration as the lower part of the shrine. The decoration with vertical scrolls is beautiful in detail, but on the whole the decoration is a little stiff and heavy in character. In the centre of the northern side of the hall, a fascinating climax with many scrolls and a decorative shrine of special design is reached.

The open hall is exciting, not only because of its size and beautiful architecture but, very surprisingly, also for figure sculpture. The top of its parapet-wall consists of a slanting seat-back, and on the outside of this seat-back the traditional panels show scenes from the Hindu epics. Nowhere else are epics found on this place. The traditional place for epics is the third frieze of the base in temples of the New kind, and there the scenes are depicted always small. Here the panels are larger, and the scenes show more vigour and life than usual. All around the open hall there are 140 panels. On the southern side, the Rāmāyaṇa is depicted in its entirety in 70 scenes; the story runs, unusually, from left to right. On the northern side the sequence of the scenes is the usual one, from right to left. First there are about 25 panels with Kṛṣṇa-stories, and next about 45 panels depicting earlier parts of the Mahābhārata.

Of the inside of the temple, the open hall offers the most exciting view. The pillars are lathe-turned without any further decoration, their shininess makes them appear as if they have been produced only recently. The under-side of the heavy parapet of the hall shows an imitated wooden rafter. All ceilings of both closed hall and open hall have a different design. The cella contains a liṅga.

2

ARALAGUPPE

Aralaguppe is a village 60 km from Hassan. The Cennakeśava-temple found here is simple in plan, but completely covered with decorative sculpture from top to bottom. It has been built around 1250 AD. In the same village there is another archaeological tourist attraction, but beyond the scope of this book: a group of plain temples from the 10th century. One of these temples, called Kallēśvara, contains a sculptured central ceiling that is unbelievably beautiful; it is undoubtedly one of the most perfect sculptures to be found in Karṇāṭaka.

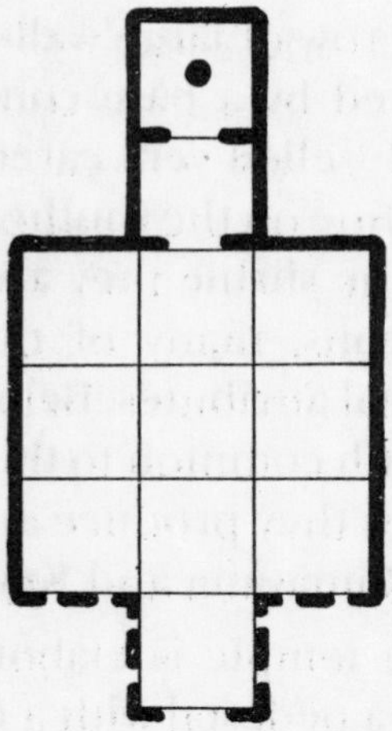

Fig. 3

The Cennakeśava-temple has one shrine and has the most simple possible plan: a shrine with nose, a closed hall and a porch.

One detail is unusual: the front side of the closed hall is open. Both this open side and the porch are provided with stone screens above the parapet-wall. Against the southern side of the shrine a coarse later addition has been built: it is a second temple, built around a venerated wall-image that is sculptured on the outside of the shrine of the old temple.

The plan of the shrine is a regular star with sixteen points. The tower is beautifully complete save for a topping kalaśa. All roofs of the superstructure here are of one single kind. First there is the very large topping roof which has the same 16-pointed plan as the shrine itself. Next there are four tiers of small roofs, all of them square in plan, many of them still topped by a kalaśa. Their shape is not very clearly visible, because each of their sides is decorated with a small sculptural panel.

The walls of the shrine and of the closed hall are also very heavily decorated, completely according to the scheme found in the New kind of temples. Below a tier of decorative towers, found between the two eaves, there is a row of large wall-images, sheltered by the lower eaves, and followed by a base consisting of 6 friezes. The decorative towers are chiselled very carefully in this temple. The wall-images are not that fine on the southern side of the hall, but on the northern side and the shrine they are excellent. Nearly all of them show Vaiṣṇava icons, many of them difficult to identify because they bear unusual attributes. Below these images there are the 6 friezes of equal width common to this kind of ornate temples; together with the images they produce an enchanting effect. The epic frieze depicts the Rāmāyaṇa and Kṛṣṇa-stories.

The interior of the temple is elaborate and fine. The cella contains a large Vaiṣṇava pedestal with a cult-image of Keśava that is too small for it, probably it is not the original one.

3

ARSIKERE

Arsikere is a small town 40 km from Hassan. The Īśvara-temple found here shows a shrine and a closed hall with exceptionally intricate architectural designs. The design of the shrine is in fact the most

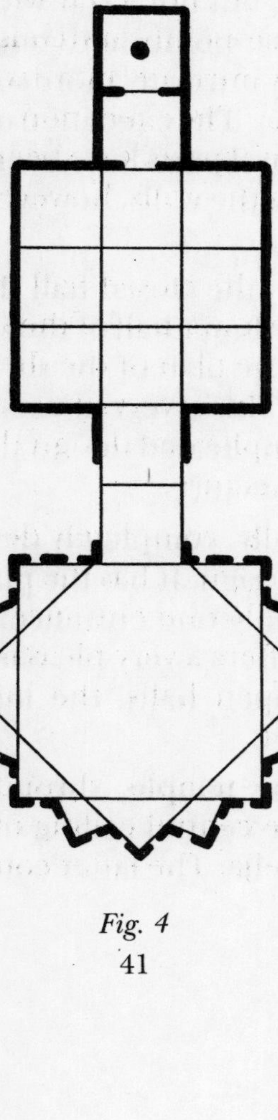

Fig. 4

complicated one found in all Hoysaḷa architecture. Figure sculpture, however, is only modest here. The monument probably dates from about 1220 AD and is in a good state of conservation.

The Īśvara-temple is a small ekakūṭa with two halls, one closed and one open. The open hall is of a completely unusual kind, because its plan is not a staggered square and because it offers no entrances to the temple. The temple can be entered through the connecting bay between open and closed hall.

The shrine is complete with tower, only the crowning kalaśa is missing. On top of its nose a bull can be found today, a recent addition with quite an ugly look. The plan of the shrine is unusually complicated: it is a star, but not a star with identical points. It has three different kinds of star-points, and consequently the architecture of all of the shrine is very intricate, more so than in any other shrine found in Hoysaḷa temples. The execution of the complicated design is fine and all architectural parts have been chiselled very well. The large images decorating the walls, however, are unusually uniform and modest.

As is often the case, the closed hall shows walls with the same character as those in the lower half of the shrine. In this temple, the hall even partly shares the plan of the shrine, because it has a star-like plan at its corners. This is very unusual, and consequently also this hall has a more complicated design than any other closed hall found in Hoysaḷa architecture.

The open hall, finally, completely deviates from the norms of Hoysaḷa architectural design. It has the plan of a 16-pointed star, is small in size and has only one entrance, consequently it has the character of a pen. It offers a very pleasant place to gather and sit because, as usual in open halls, the inside of the parapet-wall provides a seating bench.

The interior of the temple, shrouded in darkness, is very elaborate, especially the central ceiling of the hall and the ceiling of the vestibule to the cella. The latter contains a liṅga, Īśvara is an old name for Śiva.

4

BASARĀLU

Basarālu is a village near Nāgamangala, 65 km from Mysore. The Mallikārjuna-temple found here is a first class tourist attraction. It is only a small temple, but after a recent restoration it looks very fine and it has numerous sculptures of very good quality. The monument was built in 1234 AD; today it is surrounded by meadows and a modern compound wall.

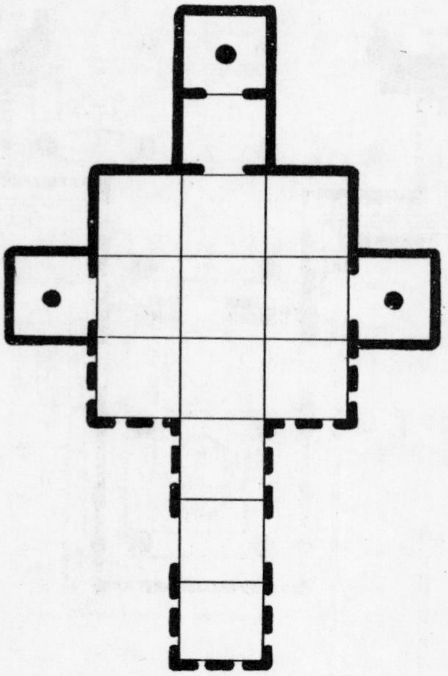

Fig. 5

The Mallikārjuna-temple is a trikūṭa, it has three shrines, but only the central one has a nose and a tower. The three shrines are

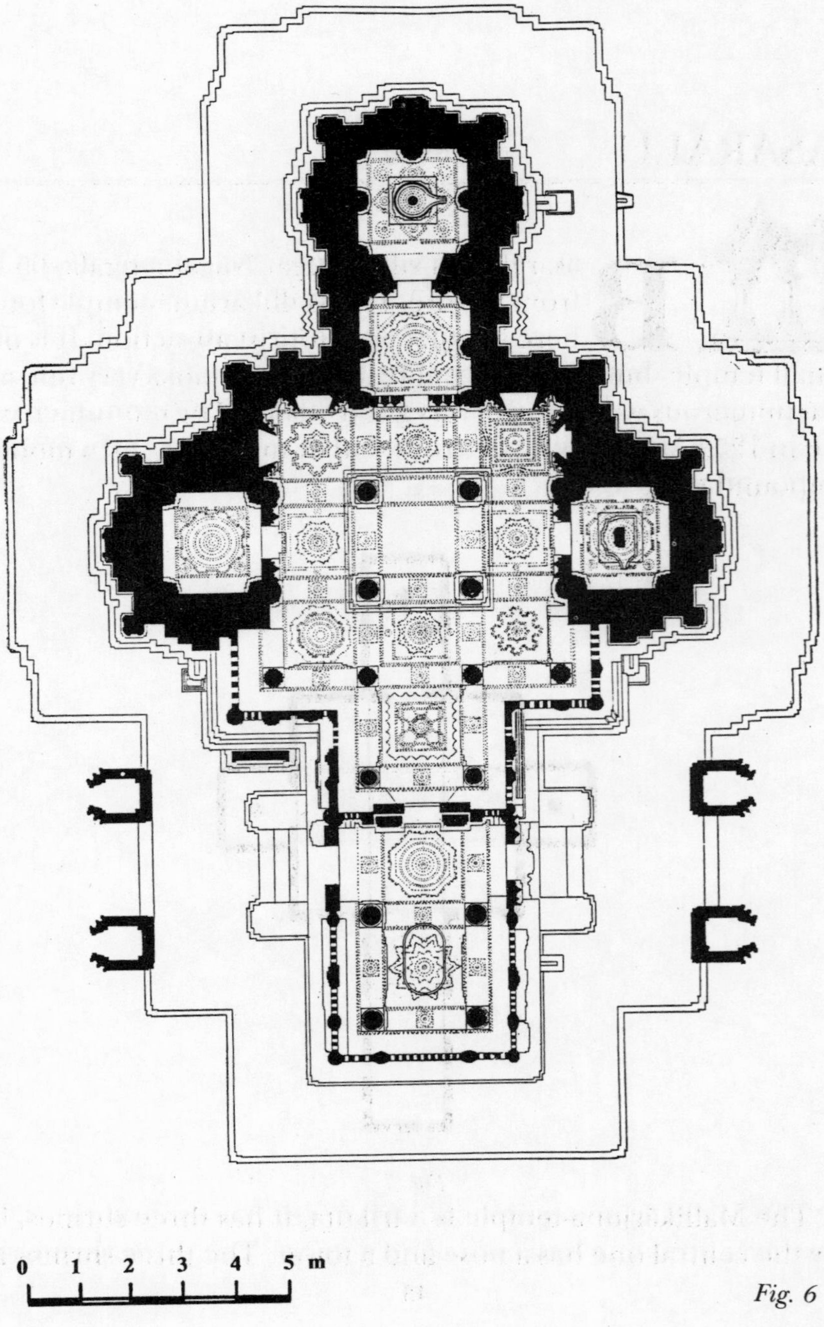

0 1 2 3 4 5 m

Fig. 6

arranged around one common hall. Inside, the central sanctum has a vestibule between cella and this hall, while the two lateral ones, devoid of a vestibule, have cellas that are connected to the hall directly. The hall is a hybrid between an open and a closed one: the back half is closed, the front half is open with stone screens between the parapet-walls and the roofing. This kind of hall is common in trikūṭas. The uncommon element in the plan of this temple is the pavilion that is attached in front of the entrance of the hall. It has the appearance of a fourth shrine but consists of open sides with stone screens and so, in fact, it is an open hall of one bay only. It forms a good unity with the rest of the building because the front of the hall is also open. Due to the added pavilion the temple has a particular and nice composition with two lateral entrances. Its beauty is enhanced by a platform that carefully follows the outline of all of the temple parts. It has two lateral flights of steps, facing both lateral entrances. A platform always adds to the splendour of entrances, simply by providing them with a flight of steps flanked by two miniature shrines.

The central shrine and its nose are complete, up to the kalaśa on top of the shrine and the Hoysaḷa crest on top of the nose. Both kalaśa and crest are very beautifully sculptured, as is the large domed roof that tops the tower and bears the kalaśa. The many miniature roofs of the tower are all finely decorated. There are three tiers of them, and the lowest tier is found all around the temple, in the other shrines and the back corners of the hall, and also in the open parts.

The central shrine and the two lateral ones all have the same simple plan: square with three projections per side. The lateral shrines only have one side complete; due to the absence of a vestibule inside, the two other sides are partly absorbed in the thick walls of the hall. Seen from the outside they do not look like shrines at all, they form a complete unity with the closed part of the hall. Of course this is mainly due to the lack of towers, but it is also due to the lack of vestibules: a vestibule causes a strong projection of a shrine out of the hall, its absence submerges a shrine in the hall.

The central shrine below its tower, the back corners of the hall and the lateral shrines all show the same architecture and decoration. The temple is of the New kind. Between the two eaves there are decorative towers, below the lower eaves there is a continuous row of wall-images. Many of these images are excellent; they are smaller and simpler than the ones found in the famous temples in Belūr and Halebīd, but often not less in sculptural quality. On the southern half of the temple many images have a special streamlined and dreamy character, one of the most beautiful ones is a depiction of Kṛṣṇa-Govardhana. On the northern side there is a very attractive Śiva-Gajāsura. As is usual in Śaiva temples all kinds of deities are depicted, including many Vaiṣṇava ones.

Below the series of wall-images, and below the screens and slanting railing found in the open parts, the base of the temple consists of 6 friezes of equal width. More than in other temples these friezes have an identical look, their carving is with much vigour and gives a similar character to each of them. In many places, the row of makaras is interrupted by a kīrttimukha, this is the face of another kind of mythological beast. In the fourth frieze the usual scroll has been replaced by decoration with lions. The epic frieze shows much force; from the left of the southern entrance to the back of the central shrine it depicts the Rāmāyaṇa, from there onwards up to the northern entrance the Mahābhārata is illustrated, and around the added pavilion Kṛṣṇa-stories and mythological scenes can be seen.

The inside of the temple is incomplete because the central ceiling of the hall has been replaced by a window, but thanks to that the elaborate interior is now more clearly visible. The central cella, with vestibule, contains a liṅga; the subordinate lateral cellas, both without vestibule, contain a cult-image of Sūrya and a pair of Nāgas. Certainly the third idol originally was a cult-image of one of the forms of Viṣṇu, because the Nāgas stand on a Vaiṣṇava pedestal. Śaiva trikūṭas with the two minor sanctums dedicated to Viṣṇu and Sūrya are not unusual among Hoysaḷa temples.

5

BELŪR

Belūr is a small town 40 km from Hassan. The Cennakeśava-temple found here is one of the most famous tourist attractions of Southern India, and it also is a favourite object for Vaiṣṇava pilgrimage. The temple is very remarkable for its size and for its elaborate sculptures. However, it also has two serious drawbacks: the open hall is closed with stone screens and the shrine has lost its tower. Notably the loss of the tower is most regrettable, because it conceals the revolutionary architectural character of the temple. The monument was commissioned by the Hoysaḷa king Viṣṇuvardhana ("prosperity of Viṣṇu") after a very important military success, and was consecrated in 1117 AD. Today it is found in a compound with an entrance gate built in later times. Inside the compound there is a second temple of equal architectural merit as the Cennakeśava-temple, it is only smaller and nearly without decoration.

The Cennakeśava-temple is just an ekakūṭa, a temple with one shrine only, and added on to the shrine it has a vestibule and an open hall. This is an ordinary plan for a Hoysaḷa temple; it is the sizes that make the plan extraordinary. Usually, a shrine measures 5 by 5 metres, but here it measures 10 by 10 metres. Usually, an open hall has 13 bays, but here it has 60 bays. The plan of the temple is underlined by its platform, which carefully follows the staggered plan of the open hall and the star-shaped plan of the shrine.

After entering the compound through a beautiful gateway (gopuram) in a later South Indian style, the visitor sees the front side of the open hall; the shrine is not visible from there. Most striking are the staggering of the hall, the perforated stone screens

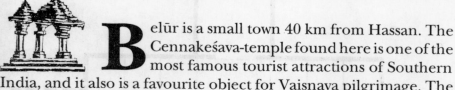

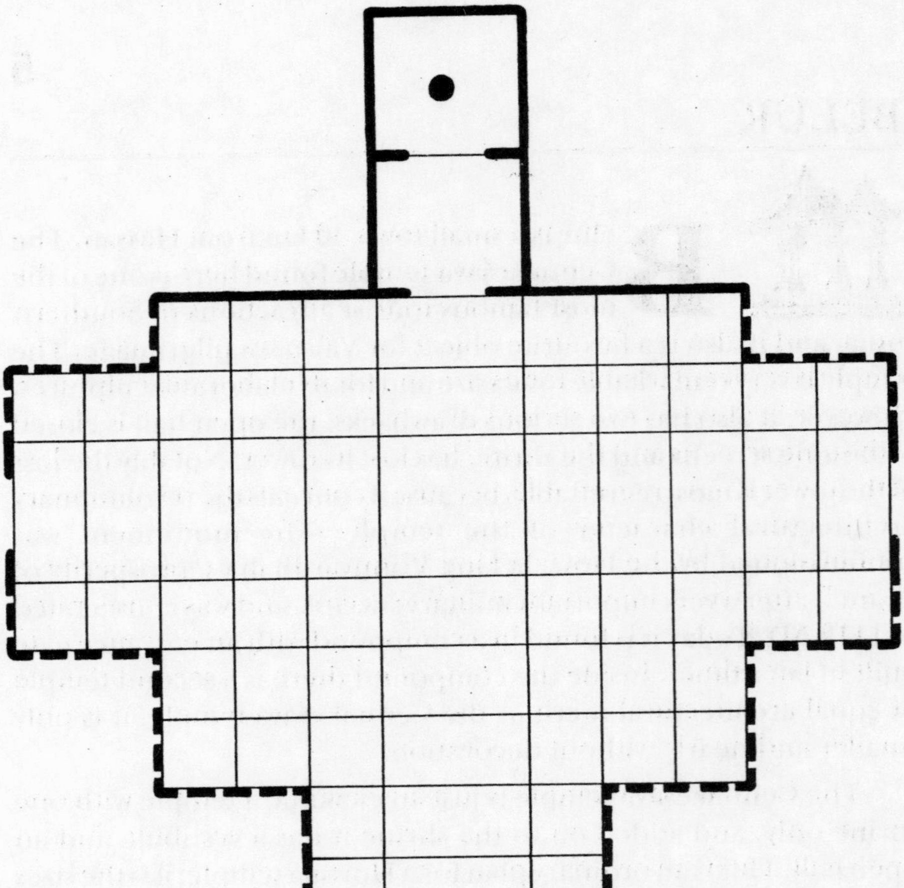

Fig. 7

and the platform. The stone screens are a later addition, they were added about 50 years after the completion of the temple. Originally, the space between the round pillars was completely open. Consequently, the fantastic interior of this giant hall was much better visible and enjoyable than it is today. The interior of the hall is definitely the most beautiful and elaborate one found in Hoysaḷa architecture and, perhaps, in all medieval Indian temple architecture. The many pillars show a large diversity in designs. The same is the case with the many ceilings. The four central pillars and the central ceiling are, of course, the climax, not only due to their elaboration but also because of their size. But all this beauty is now shrouded in darkness. Obviously, the devotees in Hoysaḷa times preferred a darker and more mysterious atmosphere than an open hall offers, and so they decided to close it off with the stone screens. In later Hoysaḷa temples with open halls, these screens have been incorporated into the original design.

In themselves, the added screens are very beautiful; many of them are decorated with very fine and lively sculpture. Below the screens there is a thick wall, it is a parapet-wall more than 2 metres high, decorated with sculpture that often resembles metal work: the special kind of stone used for Hoysaḷa temples, potstone, makes this possible. The extreme in this kind of sculpture is found in the world-famous mandanakai, found between the eaves of the hall and the top of the round pillars. There are about 40 of them; each is a sculpture of a most wonderful character, defying the properties that stone usually has. Their secret is that potstone is soft when quarried and, in the course of time, becomes very hard when exposed to the air.

The giant shrine is situated at the back of the hall. Each side of it measures 10.5 metres, and each side shows five vertical sections: a large double-storeyed niche in the centre and two heavy pillar-like sections on both sides of that niche. The two pillar-like sections adjoining the niche are rotated along their vertical axis, thus producing a star-like plan. Each pillar-like section, and also the recesses in between them, bears large wall-images of a very beautiful hybrid style. These images are the forerunners of the typical Hoysaḷa sculptures found in so many other temples. This temple was the very first important Hoysaḷa temple to be built, and consequently the Hoysaḷa style of sculpture is seen here in an early stage of formation. The large images number about 60 and show both Śaiva and Vaiṣṇava icons, which is unusual for a Vaiṣṇava temple. Particularly impressive are the depictions found on the south-western corner: a Narasiṁha on its southern side and a Śiva-Gajāsura on its western side.

Today the shrine is without tower, but from the architectural character of the walls the original shape of the tower can be inferred. In this shrine the projections of the walls are not framed by long, slender pilasters, but are given the shape of heavy pillars. The base of the shrine does not contain the traditional horizontal mouldings. From these and other details it follows that this shrine did not have the usual pyramidal tower but instead a so called *Bhūmija* tower of the kind that is found in the miniature shrines flanking the entrances of the hall. With that kind of tower still present, the view of the temple as a whole would be completely different.

In the cella of the temple there is a life-size cult-image of Viṣṇu as Keśava. The god is standing straight and bears his four attributes in the following order (clockwise): discus, mace, lotus-flower and conch.

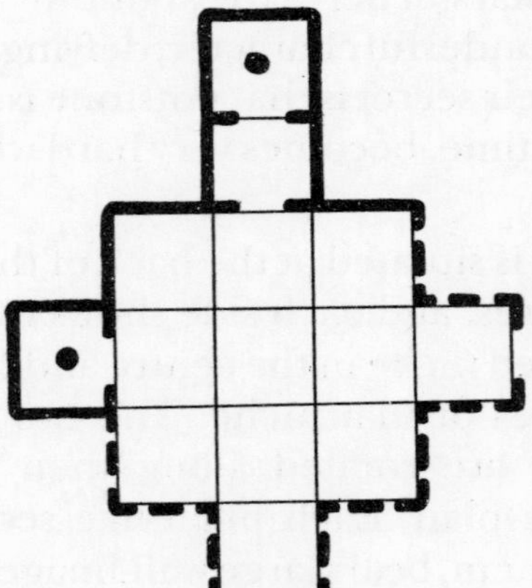

Fig. 8

To the south of the large Cennakeśava-temple there is a second temple which, although it is smaller, exhibits exactly the same remarkable architecture: also here the shrine walls lack framing pilasters, and bear no other references to architecture in wood. It has very little decoration, and at the southern side of the hall a second shrine has been added. Thus it is a dvikūṭa, a temple with two shrines. The additional shrine is just square in plan, only the main shrine has the star-like plan that is found in the Cennakeśava-temple. Like its large companion, also this smaller temple is dedicated to Keśava, but it bears the name Kappecennigarāya. It was commissioned by one of the queens of Viṣṇuvardhana, to celebrate the same victory that gave rise to the construction of the large temple.

Compared to its sumptuous neighbour the Kappecennigarāya-temple is modest, but from the architectural point of view it is of equal interest. All other buildings within the Cennakeśava-compound are of little significance from the architectural point of view, but some of them show very fine and typical Hoysaḷa sculptures.

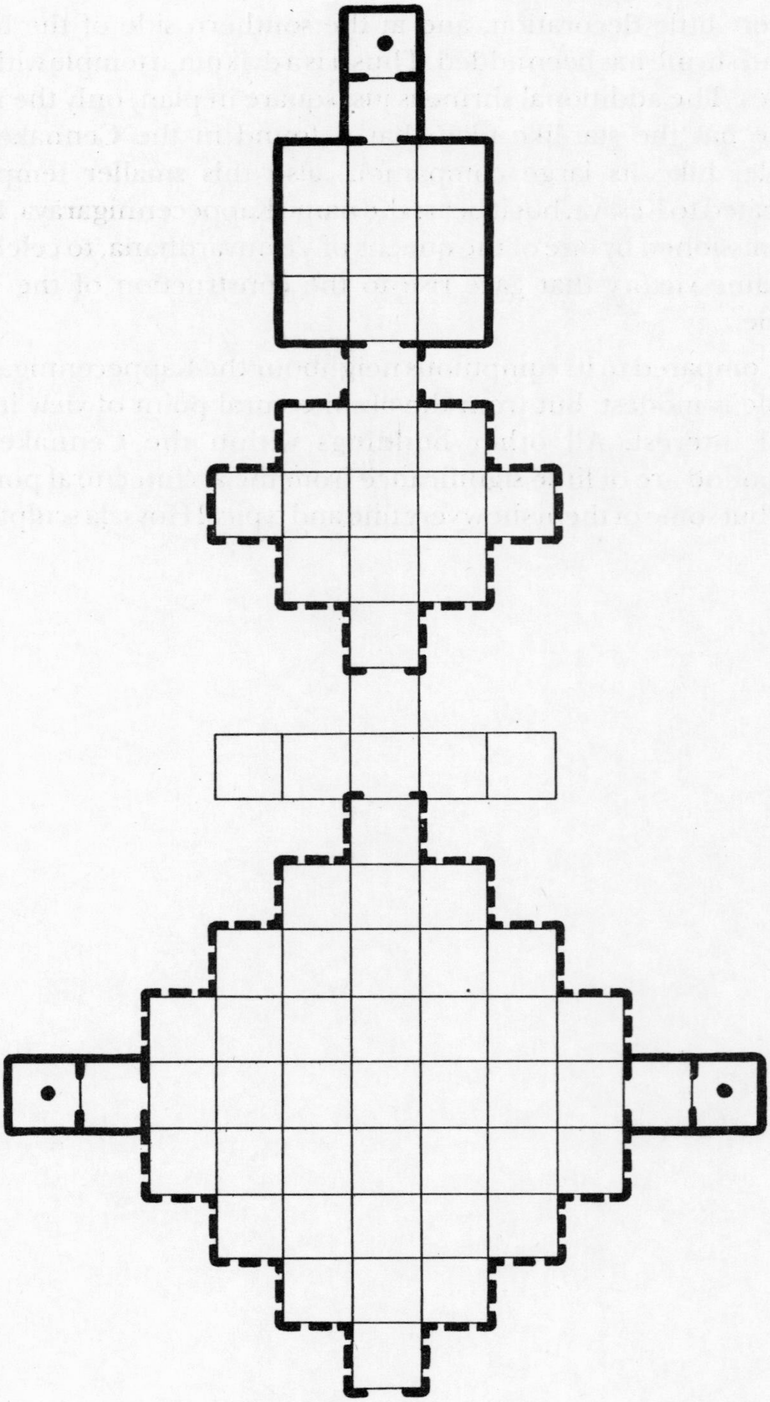

Fig. 9

6

BELVĀDI

Belvādi is 10 km from Halebīd. The Vīra-nārāyaṇa-temple found here has a daring design and is fully complete. It comprises three shrines, each with a complete superstructure, and a very vast open hall of 59 bays. After the famous temples of Belūr, Halebīd and Somanāthapur, this Hoysaḷa temple is the most impressive one for a tourist visit. It also nicely complements a visit to Belūr and Halebīd, because the impressive element here is architecture instead of sculpture. The temple has been built around 1200 AD and is carefully maintained by the Archaeological Survey of India.

The Vīranārāyaṇa-temple is a trikūṭa with an uncommon plan. Usually, in a trikūṭa, the three shrines share one small common hall, but here the two lateral shrines are attached to the lateral sides of a large open hall. Thus the front view of the temple is very impressive, because it shows a broad hall and the sides of two complete shrines facing each other. Behind this large open hall a complete temple with a small open hall, a closed hall and a third shrine is found. Obviously, the whole has been built in two stages: firstly an ekakūṭa with two small halls, later on followed by a vast open hall with two additional shrines. Between these two parts a transversal strip of five bays without any purpose or meaning is present, it clearly is part of an abandoned design.

The oldest part of the temple, showing the sequence shrine-nose-closed hall of 9 bays-open hall of 13 bays, is a perfect example of Hoysaḷa architecture. Everything is present in its most simple form, complete and undamaged. Notably the most simple forms of the two different kinds of hall are seen here side by side. The shrine also has the most simple plan: square with three projections per side. The walls are of the Old kind but are devoid of any decorative sculpture, showing nude projections framed by long and slender pilasters. Only the topping miniature roofs are finely decorated; there are three tiers of them crowning the shrine, two tiers crowning the nose and one tier crowning the walls of both halls.

The later part of the temple is the most bold extension imaginable: an open hall of 59 bays with two lateral shrines, the latter both with tower and nose. The hall is the most impressive one found in Hoysaḷa architecture, simply because of its extensiveness. And the two shrines are the most instructive ones found in Hoysaḷa architecture, because one of them is square in plan and the other star-like in plan. Star-shaped shrines are one of the characteristic features of Hoysaḷa architecture. Here we can see very clearly the difference between the two plans, because otherwise both shrines have an identical character. Their size, decoration and finish are exactly the same. The southern one is square with three projections per side. The northern one is a star with two rotated elements per side. Each visitor should look for himself to judge the effect of this difference; notably in the superstructures the consequences are large.

The noses of the two shrines are different too. The nose of the southern one is simply square in plan, the nose of the northern one is a star; not a star with all of its points identical but one with sharp points and star-shaped elements alternating. The difference is clearly visible from the ground, but still better from the roof of the large hall. This roof can be reached by a flight of steps at the southern end of the transversal strip between the two open halls. No visitor with interest in architecture should miss this opportunity to have a close look at the superstructures of the shrines and their noses.

Sculptural decoration in this temple is very fine in all the superstructures. On the walls, however, it is not first rate. The large images decorating the walls of the two lateral shrines are nice when seen from a distance, but taken individually many of them are less satisfying. Many others, though, are fine, for instance the Kṛṣṇa dancing on the snake Kāliya found on the southern side of the southern shrine, and also the admiring Garuḍa to his left; all images on this shrine side are better than most of the others.

As in all Vaiṣṇava trikūṭas, each of the three cellas contains a form of Viṣṇu. The central cella has a cult-image of Nārāyaṇa, the southern one a cult-image of Veṇugopāla (Kṛṣṇa playing the flute) and the northern one a cult-image of Yoganarasiṁha.

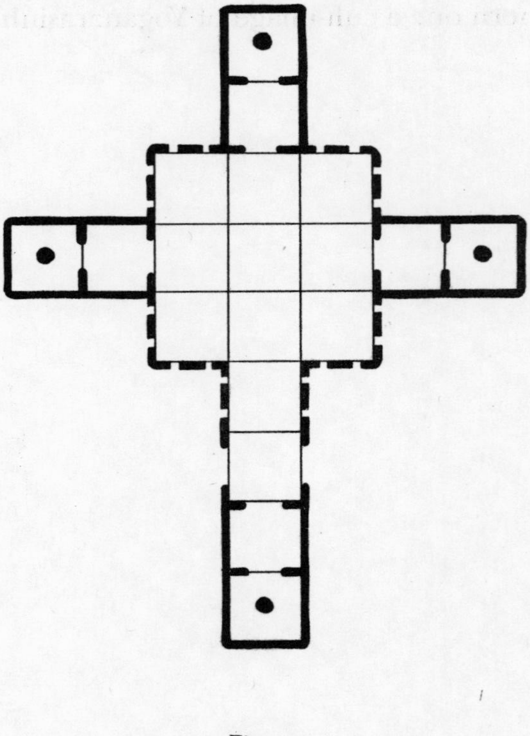

Fig. 10

7

DODDA GADDUVALLI

Dodda Gadduvalli is about 20 km from Hassan. The Lakṣmīdevī-temple found here is a small and modest monument, placed in the centre of a walled courtyard that forms a perfect unity with the temple. Embedded in the walls, four small shrines are placed at the corners of the courtyard. It especially is the fine ensemble that makes the temple very rewarding for a tourist visit. The monument dates from 1113 AD and is situated in rural surroundings on the shore of a tank.

The plan of this small temple is an exceptional one, because it has four shrines placed around a common centre. Three of them share a small open hall, and at the fourth side of this hall there is an oblong extension providing two lateral entrances to the temple and connecting it with shrine number four. All shrines have a nose and, inside, a corresponding vestibule, but the fourth shrine only has a small one with thin walls. The latter is exceptional, for it is rare in Hoysaḷa architecture that temple parts are only half-present. Also the hall is exceptional here, for it is open and nevertheless has a square ground-plan: because all four of its sides have temple parts attached to them, no staggering side remains.

Only a few metres from the main temple there is a fifth shrine; together with its vestibule it stands free and faces the south. Though coarse in execution it belongs to the original design of the ensemble. It is dedicated to Bhairava, a terrifying form of Śiva. Not seldomly a separate simple Bhairava shrine like this one is added to a temple; mostly it is so simple as to have no superstructure at all, but here it has a tower and a nose, both of them complete with kalaśa and Hoysaḷa crest.

Finally there are still four more shrines, small ones situated in the corners of the courtyard, with two of their sides embedded in the compound wall. Also these four shrines each have a superstructure, complete with kalaśa and Hoysaḷa crest. The plan of the ensemble is completed by two entrances across the surrounding walls: in the eastern wall there is a large one, which is a complete building similar to an open hall, and in the western wall there is a small one, being a framed opening only. The overall character of the ensemble described now is very fine, the more so because the pavement of the courtyard is of the same kind of stone as all the elevated parts.

Altogether the ensemble shows nine towers, all of them with nose, and all of them crowned with kalaśa and Hoysaḷa crest. Eight of these towers are of the same simple kind, they simply consist of a pyramidal pile of dented horizontal mouldings. This kind of tower is called *Phāṁsana,* and can be found all over Karṇāṭaka in simple temples. Only one tower is different, the eastern one of the main temple. It is in this eastern shrine that we come across the elaborate kind of tower usually found in Hoysaḷa temples, consisting of tiers of miniature roofs. Naturally it is this elaborate shrine that is the main shrine of the temple, it is dedicated to Lakṣmī. The architecture and decoration of the walls of the temple are of the Old kind; they show, however, no figure sculpture, only decorative towers on pilasters.

The interior of the temple is sensational because, immediately beside the entrances, guarding the separate northern cella, two demonic living corpses (*vetālas*) are found. This northern cella contains a cult-image of Kālī. The other three cellas, connected by their vestibules directly to the central open hall, contain a cult-image of Lakṣmī, an empty Vaiṣṇava pedestal, and a liṅga.

8

HALEBĪD

Halebīd is 30 km from Hassan and 15 km from Belūr. Hoysaḷa temples are especially famous for their sculptures and it is here, in the large Hoysaḷēśvara-temple, that their most glorious achievement in the field of sculpture can be found. No other temple in India shows the complete Hindu pantheon in such a lavish and successful way. However, from the architectural point of view, the temple is less successful, because all of its superstructures are missing. It was built between 1120 and 1150 AD, and is today one of the most celebrated tourist attractions in Southern India. About 0.5 km to its south there is a group of Jaina temples and beyond them, to the east, a second Śaiva temple, named Kedārēśvara, that is also very important for tourism. Here also superstructures have disappeared, but its sculptures are very rich and only second to those of the Hoysaḷēśvara-temple nearby. Naturally it has always remained in the shadow of its large neighbour. Finally, about 2 km further south, there is an unknown but very beautiful religious pond, situated in a hamlet called Hulikere.

The plan of the Hoysaḷēśvara-temple is both simple and ingenious: its two shrines lie side by side, both have an open hall in front of them and these halls are connected to each other, thus forming one larger open hall of double width. Consequently, this temple simply consists of two Belūr temples lying side by side and forming a Siamese twin. Sizes are smaller than in Belūr, but they are still much larger than those found in average Hoysaḷa temples. From the inside, the structure of a double temple is easily visible. Not so from the outside, because the numerous projections and recesses found in the back of the temple obscure its plan. This

Fig. 11

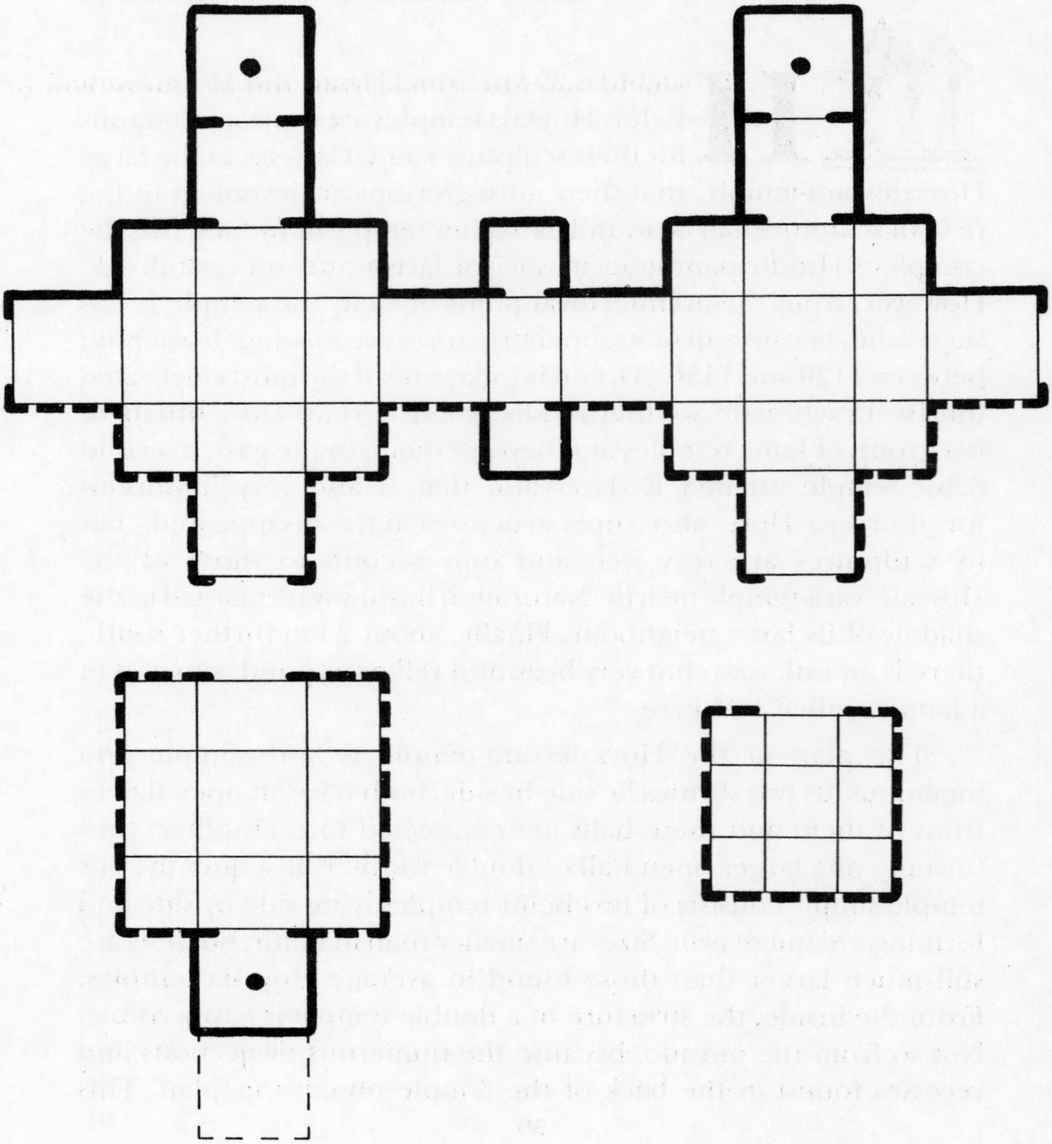

would be different if the two shrines had their usual towers, but these are missing. Consequently, seen from a greater distance, the monument looks rather shapeless and it is even not very clear which side is its front. Visitors should note that today access is from the north while the temple is facing east. The steps leading up to the platform are at the lateral sides of the temple, not at its front.

As in Belūr, the open halls were closed afterwards by stone screens. These screens are nice, but devoid of the fine figure sculpture that is found in Belūr. Also, the marvellous mandanakai found in Belūr are nearly absent here. The marvel of this temple is another one: it is the large wall-images found on the closed back of the hall and on the shrines. They form one long, continuous row of sculptures, starting at the left-hand side of the southern entrance with a dancing Gaṇeśa, and ending at the right-hand side of the northern entrance, also with a dancing Gaṇeśa. In between these two entrances around 240 images are found, producing the most lavish view found in Hoysaḷa architecture. Since the back of the temple has so many projections and recesses the view of so many sculptures is not at all dull, but is instead overwhelming. All of the Hindu pantheon is depicted here in a sumptuous sculptural style, in all India second to none in wealth and splendour. Every visitor will be impressed.

The two shrines have a star-like plan with large niches added in the centre of each of their sides. The absence of their towers is most regrettable. It is, though, not difficult to imagine what the shrines should look like, because in several other temples with similar shrines the towers have been preserved. Here not only the towers and their noses, but also all other usual superstructures, consisting of a row of miniature roofs above the upper eaves of the halls, are missing.

All around the temple, below the screens and below the large wall-images, a base consisting of 8 friezes of equal width can be found. This kind of friezes occur for the first time here in this temple, they are a radical break with tradition; conventionally the base always consisted of five horizontal mouldings of different shape. For more than 50 years these new friezes would not be taken over in any other temple, it was only in the proceeding century that this kind of base became usual in a most ornate kind of Hoysaḷa temples, which in this book are referred to as "New kind". Here in Halebīd the friezes are 8 in number and show an inexhaustible amount of figure sculpture, notably the third frieze from above, which contains scenes from the two large Hindu epics and from Hindu mythology. But all the other friezes are also amazing, both for the quality and the quantity of their sculpture. The epics cannot be followed here as two continuous stories; their episodes are mixed up and intermingled with many other depictions.

The most delicate sculpture in the temple is found in the lintels over two of the doorways. There are four doorways, one northern, two eastern and one southern. It is in the southern one of the two eastern doorways, and in the southern doorway, that the lintels show the most detailed sculpture found in the whole temple.

In comparison to the outside, the inside of the temple is simple; decorations are limited to some important places and not covering every corner. Thus, contrary to the case of Belūr, it is not that regrettable that the open side of the hall has been closed off by screens. Most striking are the four magnificent central pillars in each half of the hall, and they very emphatically clarify the plan of the temple. Inside each of the cellas there is a liṅga.

Opposite the two eastern entrances of the temple there are two large pavilions housing giant images of Nandi, the bull of Śiva. They share the same platform with the temple, but nevertheless only form a poor unity with it, because they are improvised constructions without a clear architectural character.

The second temple in Halebīd, the Kedārēśvara-temple, is a trikūṭa, a temple with three shrines. It has a usual plan: the central cella is connected to the hall with a vestibule, the two lateral cellas are directly connected to the hall. Consequently, seen from the outside, the lateral shrines look like parts of the hall. The front of

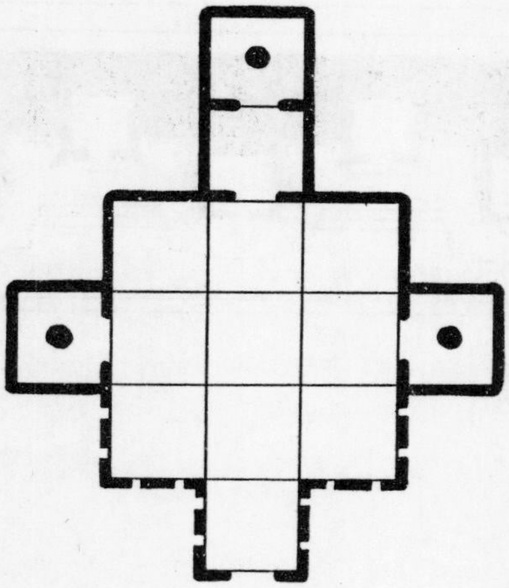

Fig. 12

the hall is open with screens. The temple is larger than average and it stands on a platform with three flights of steps, one frontal flight leading up to platform and entrance, and two lateral ones leading up to the platform only.

Besides being the only shrine with a nose, the central shrine is also the only one with a special plan: it is a regular 16-pointed star. Its superstructure is gone; it was lost during a restoration of the temple about a hundred years ago, a photograph made in 1886 still shows a large part of it. The plan of the two lateral shrines is square with five projections per side. In fact, a regular 16-pointed star also is a plan with five projections per side: in between two corners, there are three projections of the same width, but rotated along their vertical axis.

As in the large Hoysaḷēśvara-temple, the attraction of this temple especially is its large wall-images. They number about 160, and they are larger and richer than in any other Hoysaḷa temple save the Hoysaḷēśvara. As in all Śaiva temples, both Śaiva and Vaiṣṇava

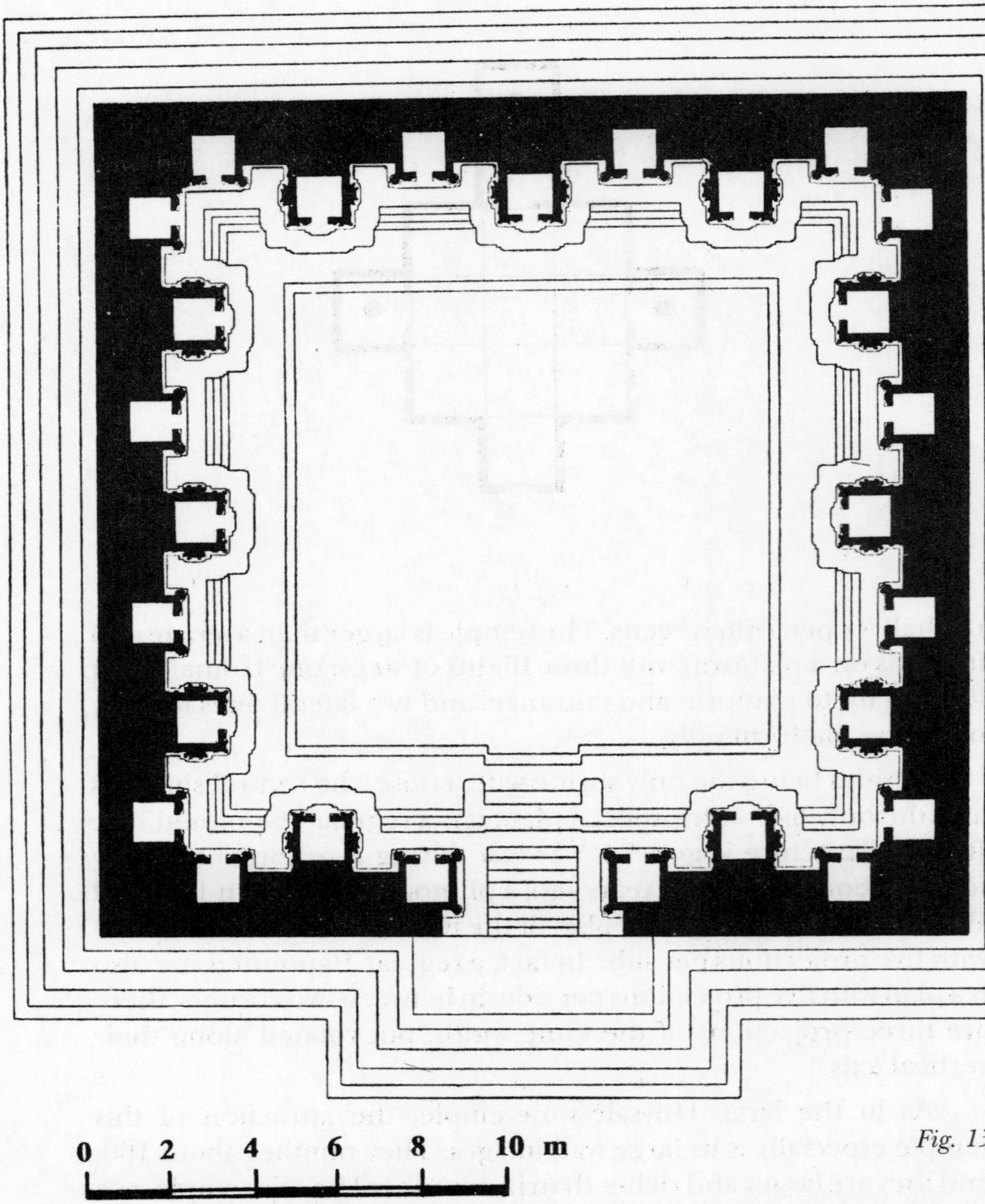

Fig. 13

icons are depicted, and so iconographical variety goes hand in hand with sculptural mastery. Lovers of figure sculpture should plan a stay of several hours here. On the southern lateral shrine some of the images have been mixed up as a result of poor restoration.

The religious pond in Hulikere is a unique structure within Hoysaḷa architecture. Only one other Hoysaḷa religious pond is known, it is located in the north-eastern corner of the Cennakeśava-compound in Belūr. That pond, however, is completely plain, it consists of a funnel of steps only. The one in Hulikere is marvellously decorated with small shrines and niches, positioned very elegantly between two landings in the funnel of steps. The view is very nice and a walk around the two landings inside the pond is a wonderful experience.

9

HĀRANHALLI

Hāranhalli is 35 km from Hassan. Two ornate temples are found in this village, one Śaiva and one Vaiṣṇava, named Sōmēśvara and Lakṣmīnarasiṁha. They do not lie side by side, but are positioned several hundreds of metres apart. The Lakṣmīnarasiṁha-temple is the most beautiful of the two, it is complete and it is without any later additions. The Sōmēśvara-temple is also complete, but it is not so

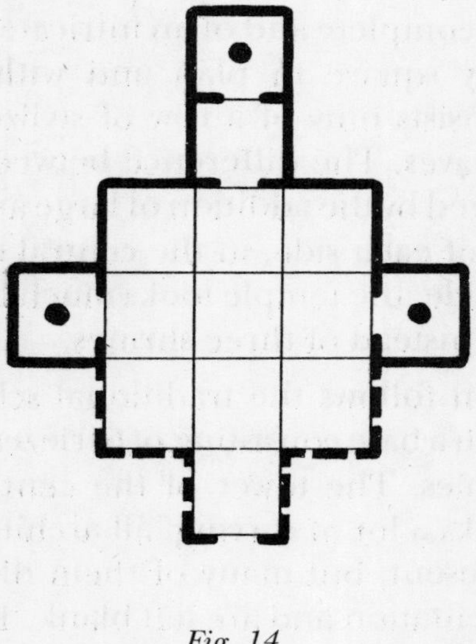

Fig. 14

well preserved and today looks a little slovenly. Both monuments date from about 1235 AD.

The plan of the Lakṣmīnarasiṅha-temple is a common one, it is a trikūṭa with three shrines situated around a common hall and a strong emphasis on the central shrine. The central shrine has a tower and a nose, the two lateral shrines are devoid of both and, from the outside, they look like they are part of the hall. The front of the hall is open with screens. The platform, of course, has a central flight of steps leading up to the entrance of the hall and also, quite exceptionally, two lateral flights of steps leading up to the platform only.

In plan and execution this temple is similar to the trikūṭas found in Hosaholalu, Jāvagallu and Nuggihalli, but only here no later structures are added on to the front of the building. This temple is complete and without any later additions. Consequently it offers a finer view than the other three temples mentioned, though its ornamentation is less in quality. The two additional flights of steps also add to the beauty of its overall view.

The central vimāna has a star-like plan and a complete tower, and also its nose is complete and of an intricate design. The lateral shrines are simply square in plan and without towers. Their superstructure consists only of a row of stylized miniature roofs above the upper eaves. The difference between the two kinds of shrine is still enlarged by the addition of large and beautiful niches, one in the centre of each side, in the central one. Consequently, seen from the outside, the temple looks much like an ekakūṭa, like a temple with one instead of three shrines.

Ornamentation follows the traditional scheme found in the kind of temples with a base consisting of 6 friezes of equal width, the New kind of temples. The tower of the central shrine misses a kalaśa and also lacks a lot of carving: all architectural parts of the tower itself are present, but many of them did not receive their traditional ornamentation and are left blank. The same is the case with the miniature roofs topping the walls of the lateral shrines and the back corners of the hall: their architectural shapes are carved very boldy, but ornamentation is lacking. Also the epic frieze in the base of the temple is left blank. The decorative towers on pilasters and the large wall-images, however, are present all around the temple. Some of the images are very fine, but a larger number of them are not. The most beautiful carving is found at the very bottom of this temple: the frieze with horses and the frieze with elephants are of outstanding quality.

The interior of the temple is very elaborate. The three cellas contain cult-images of three forms of Viṣṇu: Veṇugopāla, Keśava and Lakṣmīnarasiṅha.

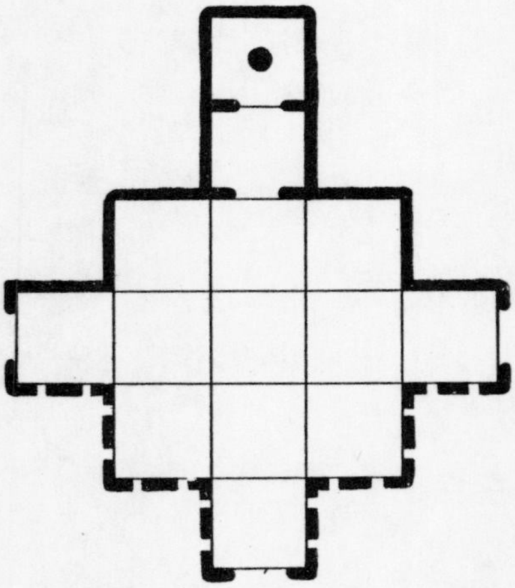

Fig. 15

The Sōmēśvara-temple is similar in plan to the large temple in Belūr: it has one shrine with nose, and an open hall with screens in front of it. Here, however, the full back half of the open hall is closed and as a consequence, when seen from its back, the temple looks like a trikūṭa with two simple lateral shrines.

The shrine has the same design as the central shrine of the other Hāranhalli temple; it has a star-like plan, a tower, a complete nose of very intricate design, and three niches. Here also, many blocks of the superstructures are left uncarved, and the carving of the friezes in the base is incomplete. The wall-images are variable in quality; a visitor with some patience, however, will find very good ones between them. Also the decoration of the upper parts of the walls is very fine in many places. But taken as a whole the temple has a slovenly look, the more so because of two ugly additions: a large stucco bull above the southern entrance and a primitive small shrine at the left side of the same entrance.

The interior of the temple is rich. The sanctum contains a linga.

10

HOSAHOLALU

Hosaholalu is a village close to Krishnarājpet, 60 km from Hassan and 45 km from Mysore. The Lakṣmīnārāyaṇa-temple found here is a fairy-tale temple, because all of the building is completely covered with very detailed, careful and monotonous sculpture. Monotony is enhanced by the very good state of conservation of all carving. The temple dates from about 1250 AD.

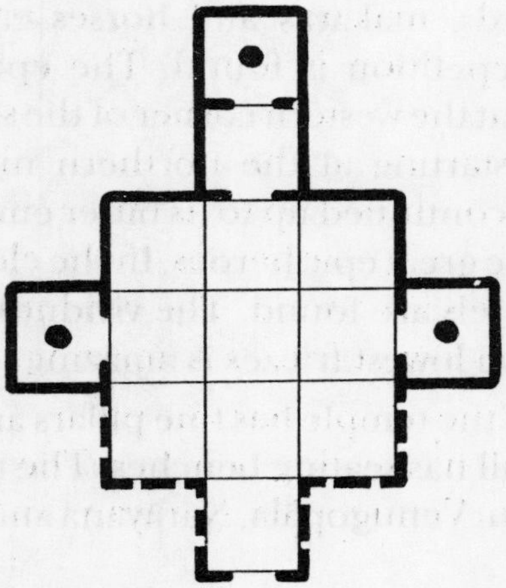

Fig. 16

The temple is a trikūṭa of usual plan: of the three shrines, the central one received all emphasis by having a superstructure, a nose, a special plan and niches. The lateral shrines are square with five projections and do not have any special feature. The front of the hall is open with screens, and here a later extension has been added to the temple. This is a pity, because now the original entrance with a flight of steps in the open is lost.

The temple is of the ornate New kind and is amazingly complete, though a kalaśa and a Hoysaḷa crest are absent. All architectural parts are present and all of them, without any exception, have received their traditional decorations. These decorations are elaborate, carefully executed and excellently preserved. The result is an amount of detailed sculpture that is too much for many visitors to digest. Nevertheless the sculptures are fine; they do not ask for individual attention, but they can stand it easily. There are about 120 wall-images in total, and most of them are nice without, of course, having the pretension of being individual works of art. As is usually the case in Vaiṣṇava temples, nearly all of the images are Vaiṣṇava. Among them are 24 depictions of Viṣṇu standing straight, showing all 24 permutations of the position of his four attributes. In the friezes the birds, makaras and horses each number about 250; here much repetition is found. The epic frieze shows the Rāmāyaṇa starting at the western corner of the southern shrine and the Mahābhārata starting at the northern niche of the central shrine; the latter is continued up to its bitter end with the merciless death of many of the great epic heroes. In the elephant frieze, many nice projecting panels are found. The vividness of the horses and elephants in the two lowest friezes is amazing.

The interior of the temple has fine pillars and ceilings, and the open part of the hall has seating benches. The three cellas contain three forms of Viṣṇu: Veṇugopāla, Nārāyaṇa and Lakṣmīnarasiṅha.

HALEBID. HOYSALESVARA.
= PARTHENON.

THINGS WE DISCUSSED
AT
AMARYLLIS

EAST FRONT: ~~LIGHT~~ HEIGHT + PLAY OF LIGHT.

WEST FRONT: HORIZONTAL + VERTICAL LINES.

BASEMENT: WAR ELEPHANTS.
HORSEMEN CHARGING.
CROCS + SWANS

SOUTH DOORWAY.

+ KEDARESVARA TEMPLE COLLAPSED

AMARYLLIS

'Dey Dreams', Karimkutty, Narikund P.O - 673 593,
(Via) Ambalavayal, Wayanad, Kerala, India
Phone: 91- 4936- 260082, +919847180244, +919847865824
Email: info@amarylliskerala.com, www.amarylliskerala.com

11

JĀVAGALLU

Jāvagallu is a village 50 km from Hassan and 20 km from Halebīd. The small temple found here is named Lakṣmīnarasiṅha, and is completely covered with relaxed and unpretentious sculpture. More than in any other Hoysaḷa temple, the sculptures have a rather folkish character here. The monument dates from about 1250 AD.

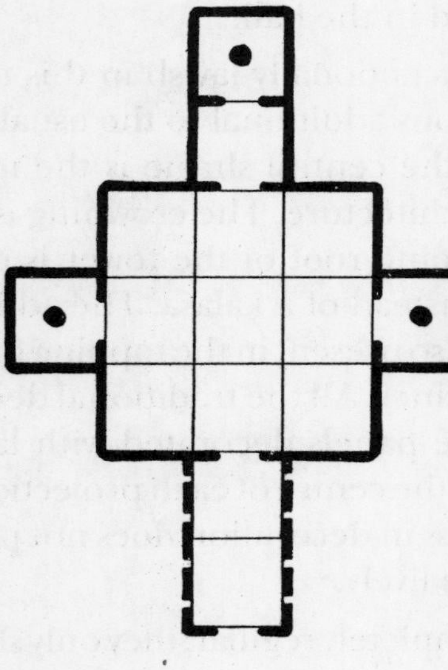

Fig. 17

The plan of the Lakṣmīnarasiṅha-temple is a common one: a trikūṭa with one central shrine with tower and nose, and two lateral shrines without towers and noses. Mostly in this type of plan the hall has an open front, but here the hall is a closed one with a porch. Today the sides of the porch have been closed off with bricks and in front of it the temple has been enlarged by later additions; consequently the original entrance to platform and temple are lost.

In other trikūṭas the difference between the central shrine and the lateral shrines is often very large. Here it is considerable, but not that large, because the plan and size of the three shrines are equal, and none of them has niches added on to them. So the only difference is the presence of a tower and a nose in the central one; in their lower parts the three shrines are identical. All three have a square plan with five projections per side. In the central shrine, these five projections are visible in three sides, but in the lateral shrines they can only be seen in one side, because the two other sides are partly submerged in the hall.

Decoration is exceptionally lavish in this temple, since in the roofs some decorations additional to the usual scheme are found. Thus, the tower of the central shrine is the most decorated one found in Hoysaḷa architecture. The crowning is the only bad thing there, the large topping roof of the tower is crowned by an ugly cylinder of plaster instead of a kalaśa. The additional decorations just mentioned are also present in the topping of the walls of the hall and of the lateral shrines. All the traditional decorations are found here, plus shield-like panels decorated with large buds and with kīrttimukhas, one in the centre of each projection of the wall below. Amazingly, this excess in decoration does not produce rigidity; the temple instead looks lively.

The walls are completely regular, they only show the decorations that are usual in the New kind of temples. The wall-images, about 140 in number, are more relaxed than usual, and also the decorative towers above them and the 6 friezes below them seem less stiffly sculptured than in many other temples. In many places there is some damage, often caused by whitewash, but it does not disturb much. This temple has a rich and relaxed character, without any pretensions. As usual in Vaiṣṇava temples, no forms of Śiva are found among the wall-images. The epic frieze, rather worn here, shows mythological scenes and the Rāmāyaṇa.

The interior of the temple is fine. The three cellas each contain a form of Viṣṇu: Veṇugopāla, Śrīdhara and Lakṣmīnarasiṁha.

12

KORAVANGALA

Koravangala is 10 km from Hassan. The Būcēśvara-temple found here is a handsome monument; it elegantly shows the characteristics of Hoysaḷa architecture and sculpture in a modest way, without

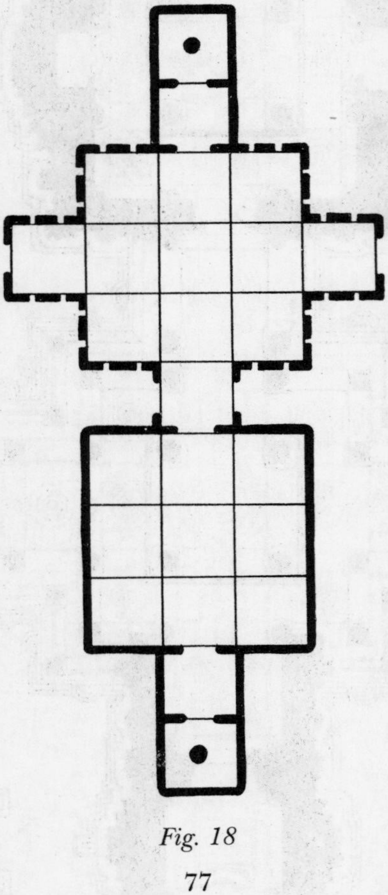

Fig. 18

Fig. 19

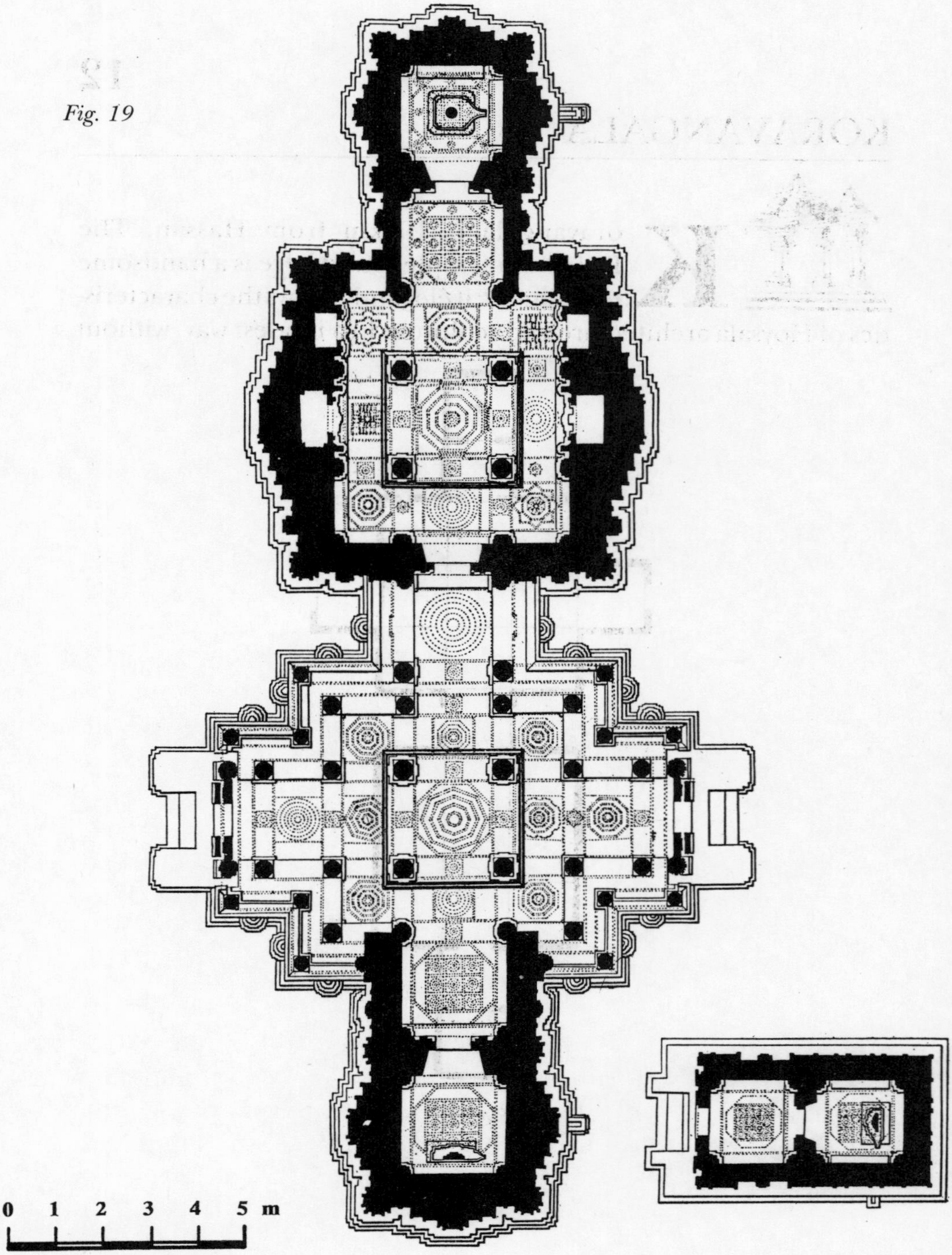

any exaggerations. It is very suitable for a tourist visit. The temple has been built in 1173 AD by a rich officer called Būci and is well preserved. Only ten years ago, cattle were rubbing themselves against its walls, but today there is a neat fence around it, and pavement and lawns, and it is guarded well. To its north, the fascinating ruins of two other temples can be found.

The plan of the Būcēśvara-temple is simple and elegant, it is a dvikūṭa with the two shrines facing each other. These shrines are connected by a succession of a closed hall and an open hall, thus presenting one of the cellas in the mysterious darkness of a closed hall, and the other in the dim light of an open hall. At the eastern end of the very oblong building, facing the south, there is a separate simple Bhairava shrine.

The western shrine facing the east is complete in every respect, and is a very fine example of a shrine of the Old kind. It is of a simple plan, square with three projections per side. Kalaśa and Hoysaḷa crest are present, and all architectural parts of the tower and the walls are decorated in the conventional way. The eastern shrine has the same plan and also has a nose, but above its eaves nothing of any superstructure is left. Even a shrine planned without tower, when complete and undamaged, should show a row of miniature roofs above the eaves. Therefore, in this case, it is not possible to say if the second shrine was planned to have a tower or not.

It is very nice to see here both kinds of hall next to each other. Both are very beautiful examples of their kind. The closed hall is complete, the open hall is not because here, again, nothing above the eaves is present. There should be the same row of miniature roofs as found above the eaves in the closed hall. The open hall provides the temple with two side entrances; both of them are framed here, and the southern entrance is flanked by two small elephants.

The decoration of the temple is of the Old kind, and is complete and fine. Notably the decoration of the miniature roofs topping the walls of the closed hall is very nice. The wall-images are modest and simple, but often they are successful and sometimes even very good. Several unusual depictions are found among them; for instance on the southern side of the closed hall, around Narasiṁha, several panels with Prahlāda and, on the eastern shrine, a chain of destruction (a chain of animals eating each other).

Of the interior, that of the open hall is the most enjoyable; it has fine ceilings and wonderful glossy pillars. The cella facing east contains a liṅga; the cella facing west, with its vestibule directly connected to the open hall, has a cult-image of Sūrya.

To the north of the Būcēśvara-temple, on the other side of a dike, there is an ensemble of two ruined temples. They are largely covered by scrub but show interesting architecture, and are very nice for more adventurous tourists to explore. Both these temples and the Būcēśvara-temple each have very large inscription slabs. These slabs disclose that the three temples were commissioned by three brothers, Govinda, Nāka and Būci, within a time span of 15 years. Būci was the youngest and was the last one to erect a temple, and he of course tried to outstrip his brothers by building the most beautiful one.

13

MOSALE

Mosale is about 10 km from Hassan. Here two small temples are found lying side by side, equal in design and execution, forming a perfect twin. Both temples are complete, and notably their superstructures show fine sculpture. The pair is very suitable for a

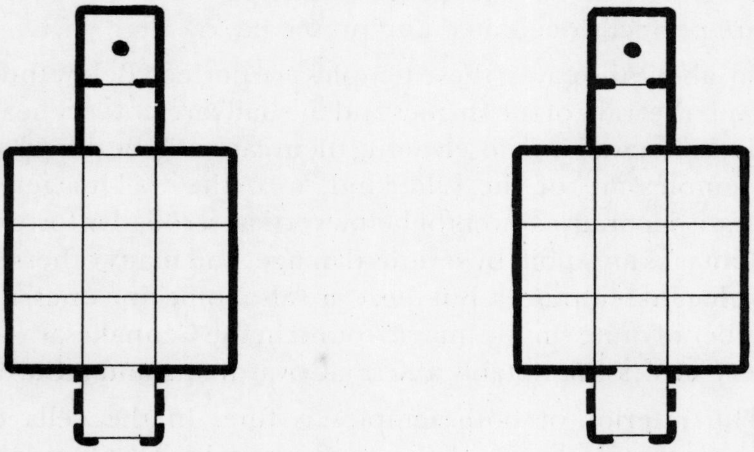

Fig. 20

tourist visit. It was built about 1200 AD and today it is found at the northern edge of the small village, in a nice rural setting.

Both temples are of a simple plan, they consist of a shrine with nose, a closed hall and a porch. The southern one is Śaiva and named Nāgēśvara, the northern one is Vaiṣṇava and named Cenna-keśava. The temples are identical and aligned, and so it is possible to consider them as a dvikūṭa, as an ensemble with two shrines. Because both shrines have a tower, the pair offers a very fine view.

The shrines are of a simple design, square with three projections per side. Their superstructures are a marvel, because they are complete and because their decoration is so successful. The two beautiful kalaśas and the two beautiful Hoysaḷa crests are the most striking, but also all architectural parts below them deserve attention, because the traditional decorations are so fine and undamaged. The same holds for the superstructures of the halls and the porches. These consist of a row of topping miniature roofs above heavy eaves, and are perfectly decorated and preserved.

So, above the eaves, these temples are perfect. Below the eaves, however, the walls of the shrines and the halls are not very beautiful, and the visitor walking closely along them can easily be disappointed. The temples are of the Old kind, with the wall-images below elaborate decorative towers or below vertical scrolls. Unfortunately, many images are spoilt by serious damage, and many others simply are inelegant sculptures. But there are also some fine ones, notably a number of quite simple images found in the Cennakeśava-temple are very successful, notably a Kṛṣṇa-Govardhana and a Garuḍa.

The interior of both temples is fine. In the cella of the Nāgēśvara-temple there is a liṅga, and in the cella of the Cennakeśava-temple there is a cult-image of Keśava.

14

NUGGIHALLI

Nuggihalli is a village 50 km from Hassan. The Lakṣmīnarasiṁha-temple found here is again a temple completely covered with sculpture. Of the group of temples of this kind, Somanāthapur included, the quality of the sculptures found here is the best. They cannot compete with Belūr and Halebīd, there we find sculptures of a royal class. But of the class of more ordinary sculpture, of the rich and heavy sculpture so typical for many ornate Hoysaḷa temples, the images and decorations found here are the most beautiful example. The temple dates from 1246 AD. There is a second temple in the village, called Sadāśiva, that has no sculptures but is very interesting from the architectural point of view: it is a Hoysaḷa Nāgara temple with a severe outside look.

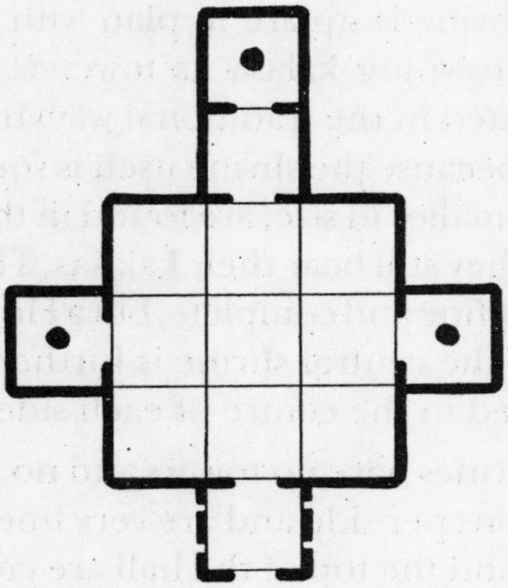

Fig. 21

The plan of the Lakṣmīnarasiṁha-temple is a common one: three shrines are situated around a common hall, the central one with tower and nose, the lateral ones without tower and without nose. Thus, in the inside, the two lateral cellas are directly connected to the hall, and only the central one has a vestibule forming the connection. On the outside, the two lateral shrines are just projections of the hall, and only the central shrine is so strongly a projection that it has the appearance of a separate building part. To this appearance adds the tower. Thus, in a trikūṭa with this plan, only one shrine is easily recognizable, and seen from the outside the temple looks like an ekakūṭa. The situation described here is found in many Hoysaḷa trikūṭas and is found here too. However, only in this temple, modern towers are found topping the lateral shrines. They do not belong there but, nevertheless, they clarify the plan of the temple.

Another later addition to the temple are the large halls in front of it. The original front is now located inside the later additions, and the original entrance has changed in character completely. Once, a flight of steps facing the porch gave entrance to both platform and temple, and the temple front offered a fine view. It is in Hāranhalli that this original situation can still be found today.

The central shrine is square in plan with five projections per side. Save for a crowning kalaśa its tower is complete, and it is excellently decorated in the traditional way. Its large topping roof is square in plan, because the shrine itself is square. Many identical roofs, only much smaller in size, are found in the several tiers of the tower, and there they still bear their kalaśas. The superstructure of the nose also is very fine and complete, but a Hoysaḷa crest is missing. The splendour of the central shrine is further enhanced by three large niches, placed in the centre of each side.

The lateral shrines have no towers and no niches, but they also have five projections per side and are very fine and complete. The top of their walls and the top of the hall are crowned with a row of miniature roofs; these stylized roofs are decorated in the same excellent way as the ones in the tower of the central shrine.

The temple is of the New kind, with walls showing a second eaves and 6 friezes of equal width. Both of the eaves are decorated very finely, and in between them the row of decorative towers is more than average in quality. Below the towers, resting on the second eaves, fine tiny figures have been added. Sheltered by the second eaves we find the row of large wall-images, here better in quality than in comparable temples. These images here number about 120 and they mainly show Vaiṣṇava icons, but also a Bhairava and a Bhairavi. In the southern half of the temple they are sculptured by a sculptor named Baichōja. His images are beautiful and they all have the same character, a character of dignity and peace. In the northern half of the temple the images are by the hand of another sculptor, Mallitamma. His sculptures are more lively and show more variation in character, but the quality of his work is less constant. It is very difficult to say which artist is the best, everybody should decide for himself. Below the wall-images the 6 friezes are found. They, of course, contain many repetitions but nevertheless do not look dull at all. The epic frieze shows only Kṛṣṇa-stories in this temple.

Inside the temple, especially the four pillars and the ceiling of the hall are beautiful. The three cellas each contain a form of Viṣṇu: Veṇugopāla, Keśava and Lakṣmīnarasiṅha.

The Sadāśiva-temple, situated to the north of the village, is an ekakūṭa of very exceptional architectural design. As in the two royal temples in Belūr, the projections of the walls are not framed by long and slender pilasters, and they also miss any other reference to architecture in wood; consequently the walls have a typically severe look. This is a Nāgara Hoysaḷa temple, complete with an exotic Nāgara superstructure crowning its shrine.

15

SOMANĀTHAPUR

The village of Somanāthapur is 30 km from Mysore. The famous Keśava-temple found here shows excellent architecture and excellent sculpture, and moreover the temple is surrounded by beautiful galleries forming a cloister. These three items together make it the most attractive Hoysaḷa temple that is left today. There are temples with better sculptures, and there are temples with better architecture, but taken as a whole this is the most impressive Hoysaḷa monument in existence. The temple dates from 1268 AD. It is one of the oldest tourist attractions in India; already in the nineteenth century it was often visited by prominent guests of the Mysore kings and by foreign officials.

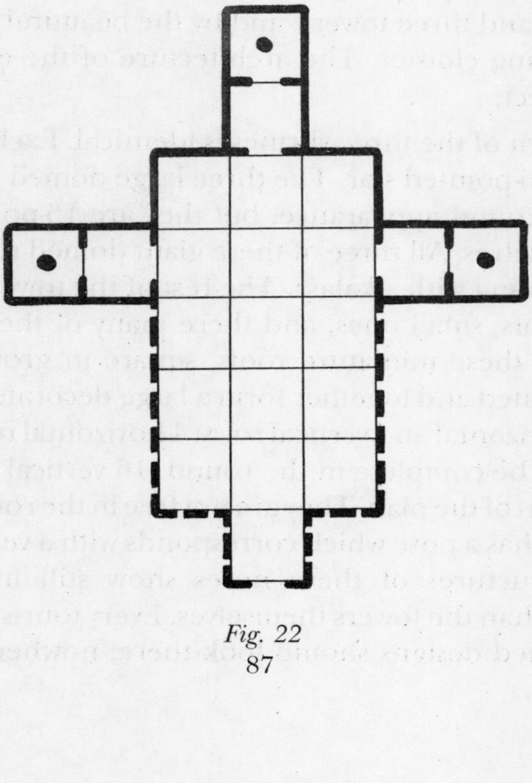

Fig. 22

The plan of the Keśava-temple is remarkable. It is a trikūṭa, a temple with three shrines, and all three of its shrines have a tower and a nose. Thus the name trikūṭa, meaning "three tops", is literally true here. In most other Hoysaḷa trikūṭas only one of the three shrines has a tower, and the two other shrines are less important and inconspicuous.

So all three shrines are of equal importance here. They are arranged around the back half of a common hall. This hall is rectangular in plan; the back half is closed and the front half is open with screens. It is the only rectangular hall found in Hoysaḷa architecture, all others are square or staggered, but also in the latter case equally wide as deep. Consequently the front of this temple offers an unusual view, not when seen exactly frontally, but when seen diagonally or laterally. Then the projection of the hall is clearly visible, showing a long unrhythmical wall, open with screens, not to be found anywhere else. But this imperfection is completely outstripped by the splendour of the back half of the temple with its three shrines and three towers, and by the beautiful platform and the surrounding cloister. The architecture of the ensemble as a whole is perfect.

The design of the three shrines is identical. Each has the plan of a regular 16-pointed star. The three large domed roofs topping them have a round appearance, but they are 16-pointed like the shrines themselves. All three of these giant domed roofs lack their original crowning with a kalaśa. The rest of the towers also consist of domed roofs, small ones, and there many of them still bear a kalaśa. All of these miniature roofs, square in ground-plan, are heavily decorated and together form a large decorated mass with a pattern of horizontal and vertical rows: 4 horizontal rows and, if the towers would be complete in the round, 16 vertical ones, one for each star-point of the plan. They are not free in the round, however; each of them has a nose which corresponds with a vestibule inside. The superstructures of these noses show still more intricate architecture than the towers themselves. Every tourist who wants to see complicated designs should look there: nowhere else on the exterior of the temple more complicated plans and decorations can be found.

The temple is of the New kind, which means that there are two eaves below the superstructures and that there are 6 friezes of equal width at the base. In this temple the upper eaves is very deep and the second one, sheltering the row of large images, is only shallow. Between these two there are the usual decorative towers on pilasters. They are very intricate and beautiful in this temple, and none of them has been slovenly executed. Below the shallow eaves there are the large images; in this temple their number is extraordinarily large, there are nearly 200 of them. Without exception they are nice sculptures, but not each of them is wholly successful: quite often they are a little uneasy and quite often they are a little stiff and lifeless. Below them, the 6 friezes are very successful, in no other temple do they produce such a rich look. The epic frieze runs from right to left and shows scenes from the Rāmāyaṇa on the southern side of the temple, Kṛṣṇa-stories on the back and scenes from the Mahābhārata on the northern side. Altogether the only weakness in the decoration of the walls is the individual quality of a number of the large images. Taken as a whole, however, the walls are extremely successful. More than in other temples the decorative towers, wall-images and friezes form a beautiful and balanced contrast, and give the walls a rich and enchanting character. The platform, following carefully the outline of the temple, and the galleries, surrounding the temple completely, also contribute to an enchanting atmosphere.

For the careful observer, a final comment on the decoration of the walls should be made. The decoration of the walls of the central shrine differs in character from the rest of the temple. In this central shrine the decorative towers are different, they are not placed above a second eaves but they are larger and together forming a shallow second eaves, and the wall-images below them are different in sculptural character. They miss the variety found in the rest of the temple and all display the same kind of elegant peace. These images are nice and polished, but they are not typically Hoysaḷa, and it is very interesting and rewarding to compare them with the images found in the other parts of the temple.

As is usual in temples dedicated to Viṣṇu, nearly all of the wall-images are Vaiṣṇava, and forms of Śiva are absent between them. The identification of many images is difficult, because they often have six hands instead of the usual four and bear unusual attributes.

Thanks to the platform, the entrance of the temple is very elegant. There are two flights of steps, one leading up to the platform, and a second one up into the temple itself. The first flight of steps is also the entrance to the platform, and invites the visitor to perform a circumambulation around the temple, called pradakṣiṇā, in a clockwise direction. Only after completing that one or more times, a visitor should go inside. The interior of the temple is very elaborate; especially the lathe-turned pillars and the intricate ceilings deserve attention. All three of the cellas have a vestibule here. The idol of the central cella is missing, there should be a cult-image of Keśava. The other two cellas contain cult-images of two other forms of Viṣṇu: Veṇugopāla and Janārdana.

LITERATURE

Brown, Percy, about 1940. Indian Architecture: Buddhist and Hindu Periods. Reprinted by Taraporevala, Bombay.

Foekema, Gerard, 1994. Hoysaḷa Architecture: Medieval temples of southern Karṇāṭaka built during Hoysaḷa rule. Books & Books, New Delhi.

Narasimhachar, R., 1917. The Kesava Temple at Somanathapur. Reprinted by Directorate of Archaeology and Museums in Karnataka, Mysore.

Narasimhachar, R., 1919. The Kesava Temple at Belur. Reprinted by Cosmo Publications, New Delhi.

Narasimhachar, R., 1919. The Lakshmidevi Temple at Doddagaddavalli. Reprinted by Cosmo Publications, New Delhi.

Nilakanta Sastri, K.A., 1955. A History of South India from Prehistoric Times to the Fall of Vijayanagar. Oxford University Press, Madras.

Settar, S., 1992. The Hoysaḷa Temples. Institute of Indian Art History, Karnatak University, Dharwad and Kala Yatra Publications, Bangalore.

GLOSSARY

bay	a square or rectangular compartment of a hall
cella	a square room with thick walls and only an entrance opening, housing a liṅga or a cult-image
closed hall	a hall with thick walls up to the roof
dvikūṭa	a temple with two shrines and, consequently, two cellas
eaves	a projecting roof overhanging a wall
ekakūṭa	a temple with one shrine and, consequently, one cella
frieze	a rectangular band decorated with sculpture
Hoysaḷa crest	the emblem of the Hoysaḷa dynasty, consisting of a royal warrior stabbing a lion
kalaśa	a sculptured water-pot, crowning the roofs of Indian temples
kīrttimukha	the face of a monster, very common in the decoration of Indian temples
liṅga	a stylized erect penis, symbol for Śiva
Mahābhārata	a large Hindu epic on the struggle of five royal brothers, the Pāṇḍavas
makara	an aquatic monster, very common in the decoration of Indian temples
New kind	Hoysaḷa temples with walls showing a second eaves and a base consisting of 6 friezes of equal width
nose	the part of the temple containing a vestibule to a cella
Old kind	Hoysaḷa temples with walls like the earlier temples built in Karṇāṭaka

open hall	a hall with only parapet-walls around it, consequently the roof rests on pillars only
parapet-wall	a thick wall with a height of about 1 or 1.5 metres
porch	an entrance shed
Rāmāyaṇa	a large Hindu epic on the struggle of Rāma
shrine	the part of the temple containing a cella
trikūṭa	a temple with three shrines and, consequently, three cellas

FIGURES AND MAPS

Figure 1. Plans of open halls. The thick dotted lines indicate parapet-walls. These halls have no full walls and, consequently, their roof rests on pillars only.

Figure 2. Amritāpura, Amṛtēśvara-temple, schematic plan. The striking element is the vast open hall, in this case consisting of 29 bays.

Figure 3. Aralaguppe, Cennakeśava-temple, schematic plan. Unusual is the open front (indicated by dotted lines) of a hall that, in all other aspects, is just an ordinary closed hall.

Figure 4. Arsikere, Īśvara-temple, schematic plan. Unique is the plan of the open hall in being a star instead of a staggered square.

Figure 5. Basarālu, Mallikārjuna-temple, schematic plan. This is a usual trikūṭa with, however, an open pavilion added to the open front. Consequently, is has not one frontal entrance but two lateral ones.

Figure 6. Basarālu, Mallikārjuna-temple, full plan (taken from the Mysore Annual Reports 1934, plate XI). The arrangement given in Figure 5 is shown here in full details.

Figure 7. Belūr, Cennakeśava-temple, schematic plan. Exceptional is the size of this temple: the small bays here are approximately of the same size as the bays in most of the other schematic plans.

Figure 8. Belūr, Kappecennigarāya-temple, schematic plan. Striking is the asymmetrical design.

Figure 9. Belvādi, Vīranārāyaṇa-temple, schematic plan. The plan of this temple is very daring, but nevertheless it consists of usual elements only.

Figure 10. Dodda Gadduvalli, Lakṣmīdevī-temple, schematic plan. Both the fourth shrine and the square open hall are special features.

Figure 11. Halebīd, Hoysaḷēśvara-temple, schematic plan. The temple itself consists of two usual ones, positioned side by side and connected by an additional bay; the facing open pavilions, however, are not regular.

Figure 12. Halebīd, Kedārēśvara-temple, schematic plan. This is a common kind of trikūṭa, but the size of the temple is larger than usual.

Figure 13. Hulikere near Halebīd, religious pond, full plan (taken from the Mysore Annual Reports 1931, plate XIII). Two landings and a circle of small shrines and niches are surrounding a funnel of steps filled with water.

Figure 14. Hāranhalli, Lakṣmīnarasiṅha-temple, schematic plan. This is a usual kind of trikūṭa with the front half of the hall open.

Figure 15. Hāranhalli, Sōmēśvara-temple, schematic plan. Remarkable is the hall in showing a staggered ground-plan and nevertheless a closed back half; exactly the same arrangement is found twice in the large temple in Halebīd.

Figure 16. Hosaholalu, Lakṣmīnārāyaṇa-temple, schematic plan. This is a usual kind of trikūṭa with the front half of the hall open.

Figure 17. Jāvagallu, Lakṣmīnarasiṅha-temple, schematic plan. This is a trikūṭa with a closed hall; the porch is unusual in consisting of two bays instead of one.

Figure 18. Koravangala, Būcēśvara-temple, schematic plan. Striking is the positioning of the two shrines (they are facing each other) and the presence of both kinds of hall (one closed and one open).

Figure 19. Koravangala, Būcēśvara-temple, full plan (taken from the Mysore Annual Reports 1933, plate X). Close to one end of the temple there is a third separate shrine.

Figure 20. Mosale, Nāgēśvara-Cennakeśava-ensemble, schematic plan. This ensemble consists of two ekakūṭas of the most simple kind, positioned side by side.

Figure 21. Nuggihalli, Lakṣmīnarasiṅha-temple, schematic plan. This is a usual kind of trikūṭa with a closed hall.

Figure 22. Somanāthapur, Keśava-temple, schematic plan. This is an unusual trikūṭa because all three of the shrines have a vestibule and because the hall is rectangular.

Map 1. Peninsular India. The Hoysaḷa temples are found within the dotted rectangle. Other archaeological tourist places in Karṇāṭaka are Bādāmi (including the neighbouring villages Pattadkal and Aihole) and Vijayanagar.

Map 2. The Hoysaḷa region in southern Karṇāṭaka. Places for orientation are given in capital letters, villages with Hoysaḷa temples are given in lower case letters. Only Shravan Belgola is a non-Hoysaḷa tourist place.

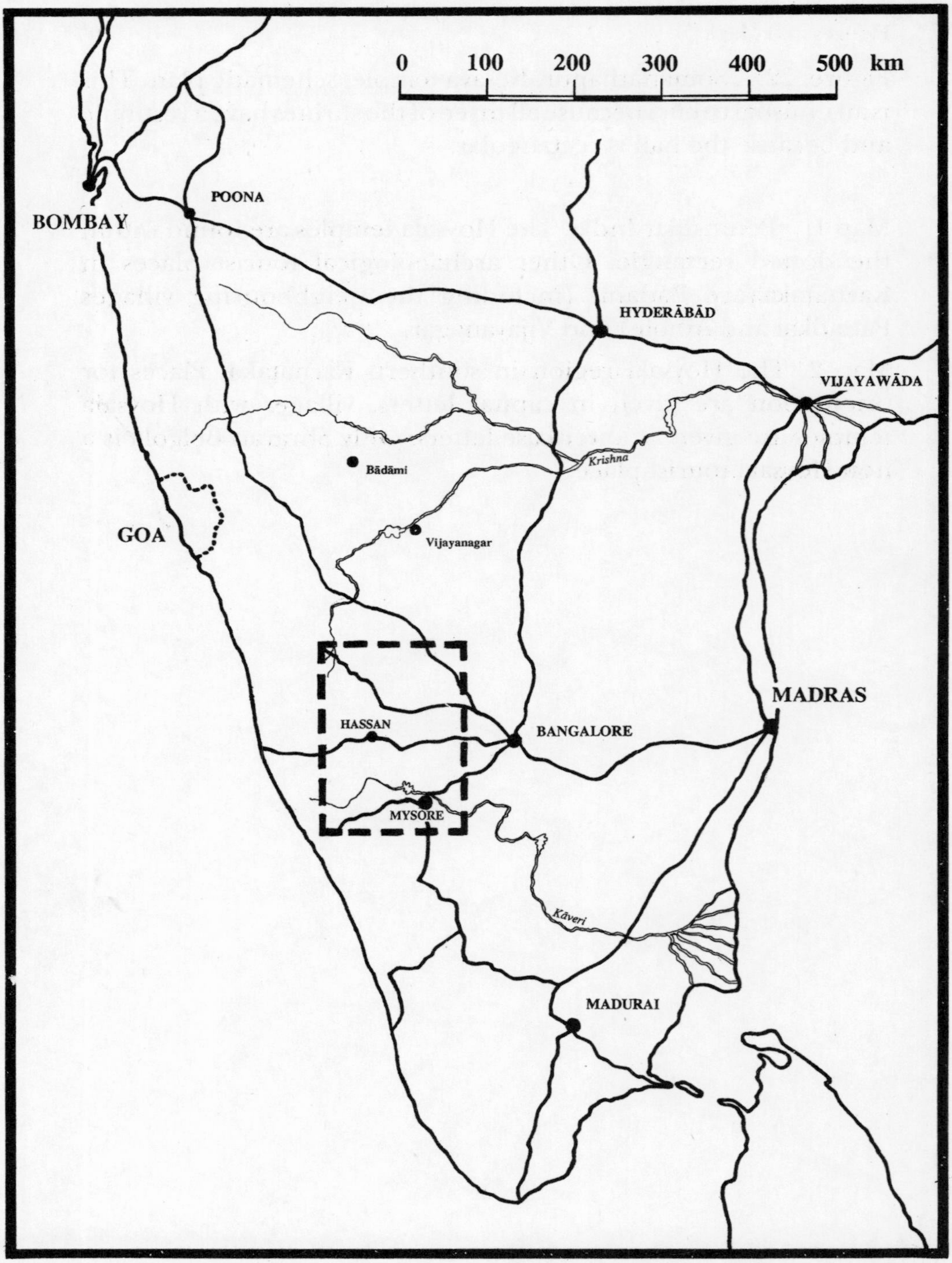

0
100
200
300
400
500 km
BOMBAY
POONA
HYDERĀBĀD
VIJAYAWĀDA
Krishna
Bādāmi
Vijayanagar
GOA
MADRAS
HASSAN
BANGALORE
MYSORE
Kāveri
MADURAI

Map 1

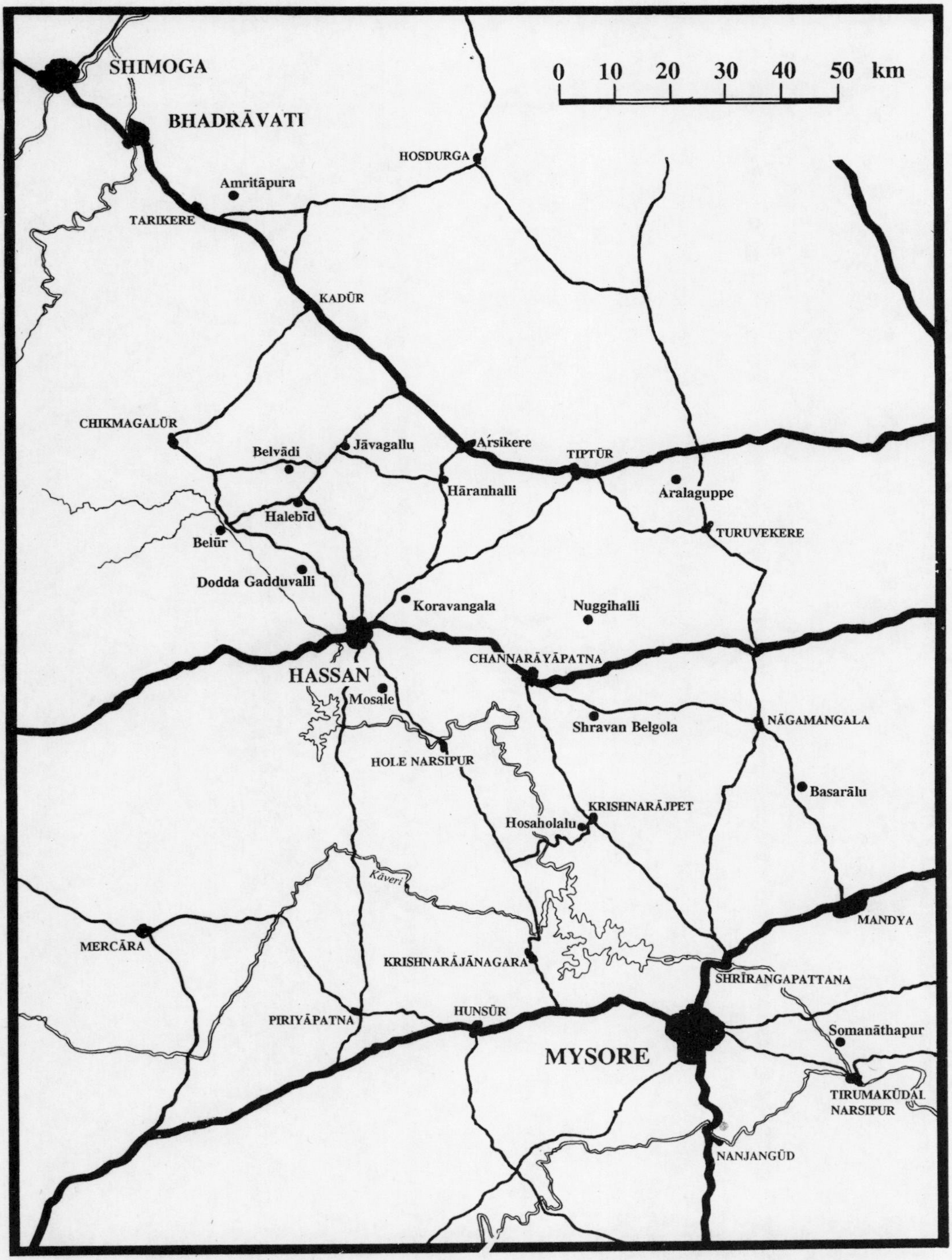
SHIMOGA
BHADRĀVATI
0 10 20 30 40 50 km
HOSDURGA
Amritāpura
TARIKERE
KADŪR
CHIKMAGALŪR
Belvādi
Jāvagallu
Ársikere
TIPTŪR
Hāranhalli
Áralaguppe
Halebīd
Belūr
TURUVEKERE
Dodda Gadduvalli
Koravangala
Nuggihalli
HASSAN
CHANNARĀYĀPATNA
Mosale
Shravan Belgola
NĀGAMANGALA
HOLE NARSIPUR
Basarālu
KRISHNARĀJPET
Hosaholalu
Kāveri
MERCĀRA
MANDYA
KRISHNARĀJĀNAGARA
SHRĪRANGAPATTANA
PIRIYĀPATNA
HUNSŪR
Somanāthapur
MYSORE
TIRUMAKŪDAL NARSIPUR
NANJANGŪD

Map 2

INDEX

Pl. 1. Amritāpura, Amṛtēśvara-temple. Side view, South.

Pl. 2. Amritāpura, Amṛtēśvara-temple. Parapet-wall of the open hall with scenes from the Rāmāyana.

Pl. 3. Amritāpura, Amṛtēśvara-temple. Two views of the interior of the open hall.

Pl. 4. Aralaguppe, Cennakeśava-temple. One of the back corners of the closed hall.

Pl. 5. Aralaguppe, Cennakeśava-temple. Diagonal back view with the star shrine prominent, north-west.

Pl. 6. Arsikere, Īśvara-temple. a) Diagonal back view with the star shrine prominent, south-west. b) Side view of the open hall.

Pl. 7. Arsikere, Īśvara-temple. The three different kinds of star-points of the shrine.

Pl. 8. Basarālu, Mallikārjuna-temple. Diagonal back view, south-west.

Pl. 9. Basarālu, Mallikārjuna-temple. Large wall-image, Kṛṣṇa lifting mount Govardhana.

Pl. 10. Belūr, Cennakeśava-temple. a) Front view, east. b) Side view with indication of the lost superstructures, south.

P1. 11. Belūr, Cennakeśava-temple. Miniature shrine with Bhūmija tower; the same kind of superstructure once crowned the shrine of the temple.

P1. 12. Belūr, Cennakeśava-temple. Lintel of the eastern doorway, showing in the centre Narasiṅha seated on Garuḍa.

P1. 13. Belūr, Cennakeśava-temple. One of the famous mandanakai, lady looking in a mirror.

Pl. 14. Belvādi, Vīranārāyaṇa-temple. Superstructure of the southern shrine.

Pl. 15. Belvādi, Vīranārāyaṇa-temple. a) Front view showing two shrines and the large open hall, east. b) Diagonal back view, north-west.

Pl. 16. Belvādi, Vīranārāyaṇa-temple. Side view of the large open hall.

Pl. 17. Belvādi, Vīranārāyaṇa-temple. Two views of the interior of the large open hall.

Pl. 18. Dodda Gadduvalli, Lakṣmīdevī-temple. a) View from outside the enclosure, south. b) Full view of the temple itself, west.

Pl. 19. Dodda Gadduvalli, Lakṣmīdevī-temple. One of the small shrines in the corners of the enclosure.

Pl. 20. Halebīd, Hoysaḷēśvara-temple. a) Diagonal back view, south-west. b) Side view, south. Both photographs with indication of the missing superstructures.

Pl. 21. Halebīd, Hoysaḷēśvara-temple. One of the back corners of the hall.

Pl. 22. Halebīd, Hoysaḷēśvara-temple. Lakṣmīnārāyaṇa, Viṣṇu with Lakṣmī seated on his left thigh.

Pl. 23. Halebīd, Hoysaḷēśvara-temple. Large wall-image, Śiva slaying the demon Andhaka.

Pl. 24. Halebīd, Kedārēśvara-temple. Old photograph dating from 1886, showing the superstructure of the central shrine that is lost today. Taken from Epigraphia Carnatica V (1902).

Pl. 25. Halebīd, Kedārēśvara-temple. a) Side view, south. b) Back view with the central shrine prominent, west.

Pl. 26. Halebīd, Kedārēśvara-temple. Large wall-image, dancing Śiva.

Pl. 27. Hulikere, religious pond. North-western corner of the funnel of steps.

P1. 28. Hāranhalli, Lakṣmīnarasiṅha-temple. a) Diagonal side view with one of the lateral shrines prominent. b) The lowest friezes of the base.

Pl. 29. Hāranhalli, Lakṣmīnarasiṅha-temple. Large wall-image, Viṣṇu as Narasiṅha.

P1. 30. Hāranhalli, Sōmēśvara-temple. Diagonal back view, south-west.

Pl. 31. Hāranhalli, Sōmēśvara-temple. One of the back corners of the hall and the superstructure of the nose.

Pl. 32. Hosaholalu, Lakṣmīnārāyaṇa-temple. Side view, south.

Pl. 33. Hosaholalu, Lakṣmīnārāyaṇa-temple. The walls of shrine, nose and hall.

Pl. 34. Hosahəlalu, Lakṣmīnārāyaṇa-temple. Large wall-image, Viṣṇu.

Pl. 35. Jāvagallu, Lakṣmīnarasiṅha-temple. Diagonal back view, south-west.

Pl. 36. Jāvagallu, Lakṣmīnarasiṅha-temple. Side view of the central shrine and its nose.

Pl. 37. Koravangala, Būcēśvara-temple. a) Diagonal side view with the western shrine and the closed hall prominent, south-west. b) The open hall and, behind it, the eastern shrine.

Pl. 38. Koravangala, Būcēśvara-temple. Large wall-images, two musicians.

Pl. 39. Mosale, Nāgēśvara-Cennakeśava-temples. Diagonal back view, north-west.

P1. 40. Mosale, Nāgēśvara-temple. The top of the shrine, crowned with a majestic kalaśa.

Pl. 41. Mosale, Cennakeśava-temple. Large wall-image, Garuḍa.

Pl. 42. Nuggihalli, Lakṣmīnarasiṅha-temple. Large wall-image by the sculptor Baichōja, Viṣṇu.

Pl. 43. Nuggihalli, Lakṣmīnarasiṅha-temple. Side view, south.

Pl. 44. Nuggihalli, Lakṣmīnarasiṅha-temple. Large wall-image by the sculptor Mallitamma, Arjuna shooting the fish.

Pl. 45. Nuggihalli, Sadāśiva-temple. Diagonal back view, north-west.

P1. 46. Somanāthapur, Keśava-temple. Front view, east.

Pl. 47. Somanāthapur, Keśava-temple. Three of the star-points of the southern shrine.

Pl. 48. Somanāthapur, Keśava-temple. Large wall-image, Sarasvatī.